TO SEE A DEAD MAN DANCE

The disturbing tale of a
terrible Lancashire murder

by Geoffrey Mather

Carnegie Press, 1989

To see a dead man dance
by Geoffrey Mather

First published, 1989
Copyright, © Geoffrey Mather, 1989

Typeset in 10pt Times Roman and Plantin Medium by Carnegie Press
Published by Carnegie Press, 125 Woodplumpton Road, Fulwood, Preston PR2 2LS Tel 728868
Printed by T. Snape & Co. Ltd., Boltons Court, Preston

ISBN 0 948789 21 2

TO SEE A DEAD MAN DANCE

The disturbing tale of a terrible Lancashire murder

In Memory of
JAMES BARTON,
Who was murdered at Back-house pit, the 2nd day
of January, 1863,
AGED 55 YEARS,
And was buried at Haigh Church.

Farewell dear wife my life is past,
My love to you through life did last,
Now I am gone no sorrows take,
But love my children for my sake.

Let friends forbear to mourn and weep,
Whilst sweetly in the dust I sleep;
A troublesome world I've left behind,
A glorious crown in heaven shall find.

by Geoffrey Mather

Acknowledgements

THIS book came to be written because of the enthusiasm for genealogy of Rosemary Grime, wife of Ian Grime, a Chorley businessman. He had been told by his father that some relative by marriage had been involved in a murder in the 1860s. She made inquiries through a records office. Was there – she asked – anyone from Chorley involved? Back came a name: Thomas Grime. Next came a search through censuses of the time. Ian Grime had a positive identification: Thomas Grime, he found, was his great grandfather's brother. The material which forms the basis of this book was then collected.

Also consulted:

Haigh Hall, and *A History of Haigh Hall*, Wigan Corporation.
Camerer Cuss Book of Antique Watches, Antique Collectors' Club.
Arthur Bickerstaffe of Samlesbury Hall.
Ian Pollard, barrister.
Robert Lawrenson, watch collector.
George Lowton, Haigh resident.
The Blackpool Story: Brian Turner/Steve Palmer.
Accrington: Chronology and Men of Mark, by R. S. Crossley.
History and Development of the Wigan Coalfield, Wigan Borough Museums Service.
Transactions of the Institution of Mining Engineers, 1957/8.
Haigh 1796/1840/1930, J. Unsworth.
The Hangmen of England/Horace Bleackley (Chapman and Hall)

Contents

The principals

James Barton	Killed as he tended boiler fires at Button Pit, Haigh, in Lancashire, then incinerated: 2/3 January, 1863.
Thomas Grime	Tried and hanged in 1866 for the murder of James Barton on his own admission of having been there at the time and the evidence of his having had in his possession the dead man's watch.
William Lamberton	Made first admission of murder, saying that seven men were involved. Found to be both drunk and innocent.
John Healey (alias Donnelly, alias McDermott)	Made second admission of murder "with four others." Retracted. Said he had been in drink and did not know where he went. Died before Grime appeared at Liverpool Assizes.
Thomas Walton (alias Patten, alias Stepper)	Made third admission of murder "with two others." Retracted. Blamed drink.
William Thompson	Implicated by Thomas Grime and arrested in Barrow-in-Furness but later freed. According to Grime he was the man who consigned James Barton to the flames of his own furnace as an act of revenge.
Joseph Seddon	Implicated by Thomas Grime as one of those present at the murder of James Barton. Died before Grime's first court appearance.

Preface

ONE and a quarter centuries ago, James Barton, fireman and engine minder at a small Lancashire pit, was brutally attacked, while on duty at night, and fed into his own furnace; dead or alive at the time, no-one knows. This was a notorious murder. Its investigation ranged over almost three years. And at the end of that time up to 30,000 people watched the hanging of a man named Thomas Grime.

This book is a closely-observed study of the trial and all that led up to it. Through it, the reader might form an opinion of whether Grime was reasonably judged.

The fine detail is remarkable – a tribute to the diligence of observers at the time. This was an age when local newspapers were often the principal source of news, both foreign and domestic. Their reporters were allowed remarkable freedom of expression and they wrote weightily and ponderously. What they did not know, they surmised; but they made plain the distinction between what they surmised and what they knew. They frequently hinted that knowledge was in their possession which they might not, in truth, have, thus giving the impression that they were all-knowing and all-seeing. It was more vanity than misrepresentation and the ploy is not unknown in this present age.

They worked on the assumption that righteous men were employers and administrators, people of the establishment, to be given their utmost respect, while many others – people of the streets and alehouses – were blackguards and wastrels until proved otherwise. Ministers were "reverend gentlemen".

They ranged far in their search for crime to condemn (and for a moral lesson to be drawn), and when they found it they were often more disparaging than the judge. In 1864, for instance, reporting an unremarkable murder in Leeds (a domestic stabbing where a wife lost her life), the Chorley newspaper made reference to the husband, one Joseph Myers, as leading "a dissipated life" and indulging "in low and brutalising sports"; while his house was "a miserable unfurnished dwelling." What, we might ask in this more objective age, is "dissipated"? And what, a "brutalising sport?" The condemnation lies more in what is suggested than what is stated.

Victorian reporters never merely looked at things; they "examined" them closely. They spoke of Barton's murder as a crime "that excites disgust and horror throughout the kingdom." They referred to others who guessed at the detail of that crime as "profound speculators." Unlike many present-day observers they were capable of prodigious feats of verbatim note-taking. They put words like "hypothesis" and "demonic" to their editors and actually got them printed. Newspapers were not only read from end to end, but passed on as the sole source of contemporary information.

The result of all this note-taking is as remarkable for the social habits it reveals as its true subject: the controversies and arguments surrounding a murder which, by the standards of the time, was unthinkable.

Various people confess. Thomas Grime, the one who confesses most convincingly, is the one who goes to the gallows – speeded in that process by two honest members of his immediate family who volunteer vital information. Did he take part in the attack? There is room for considerable doubt. Was he there at the time? Almost certainly he was, with others. Who, then, did it? Most likely, a friend and companion of Grime's who walked free: William Thompson. And why did he walk free? Because he showed more self-control than his friends and kept silent at the right time; and because there was no corroboration of what Grime had alleged was Thompson's part in the affair.

The reader might conclude that Thompson was helped by the inadequacy of the police. For if Grime's account is right, Thompson was stopped on the night or early morning of the murder by two policemen and, at the time, he had with him the dead man's knife and distinctive watch. They allowed him to proceed. They would not, of course, realise at that stage that a murder had been committed. Later, would they not recall that incident? And if they recalled it, why did they not report it? Could it be that they kept quiet because it might be seen as reflecting on their own judgments and competence?

There were questions about this during Grime's trial. And the police officer involved in that questioning – one Inspector Peters – said his inquiries had failed to reveal any confirmation of the incident. It seems unlikely, to a disinterested observer, that Grime would invent such a story. If it were a fabrication, why would he describe a set of circumstances in which the police were involved, and which they could, therefore, easily check?

The condemned man went to the gallows on his own confession of complicity, and on the evidence of the dead man's watch having been in his possession.

Did Grime, when he went to the pit with others on the night of the murder, intend to murder? It would appear not. Whereas Thompson would seem, at this stage, to have gone there precisely for that purpose – because he had a grudge against his victim.

Here, another point about Inspector Peters which does not inspire confidence: his loose use of words at the trial which imply that Grime admitted going to murder on the night of Barton's death, when what he actually said was that he went there, and that murder took place. The inspector did not even see a distinction between those two accounts.

Yet did not this hanged man, Grime, absolve others, including Thompson, as he waited for death? Yes he did. But he was besieged by so many religious tracts, and reminders of the hereafter, that he might well have concluded that a little magnanimity would do him no harm when he met his Maker, whatever the truth of the matter.

So much for the story as it will be told.

Running parallel with it are hints at the social practices of the time. Here we have a victim of 55, universally referred to as "an old man." We have an earl as owner of the pit where he died, always represented in court by a solicitor whose task it was, presumably, to do no more than keep the noble gentleman fully informed; a solicitor, moreover, whose name always appeared in accounts of hearings as having been present.

We are presented with a vision of a society constantly on its feet. The constable walks his prisoner, sometimes for miles, to the lock-up. Men walk 25 miles, drink, and walk again. They appear to spend in pennies and drink in gallons. They are drinking by night and by day, and if what they say incriminates them, drink is their excuse.

This constant insobriety was noted with distaste by Richard Appleton, chaplain at Kirkdale Gaol – where Barton's murder was revenged – in his annual report of 1863.

"It is a melancholy reflection," he wrote, "that within 12 months, no fewer than nine human beings were fearfully ushered into eternity in this place. I wish I could omit or modify what has been my annual complaint in every report with respect to the prevalence of habits of intoxication, and the manifold and grievous consequences to which they are daily leading in every part of our criminal district. I can hardly find a single page in my journal in which I do not see some notice or other of the sad effects of this monster vice. Here are a few, almost at random:

"Eliza Hannigan, wife of a missionary sent by the Irish Reformation Society, sentenced to one calendar month for assaulting her husband while in a state of intoxication. Eliza Hannigan, a second time for being drunk, six months, and summarily convicted, all through intemperance.

"Alfred E. Clarke, charged with forging three orders for goods – a most respectable looking young man – another sad victim of intemperance.

"Benjamin Longstaff, for trial for killing his mother. He says his father, mother and himself were all drunk together; that he himself was out of work; that his father was earning 33 shillings [£1.65] a week and yet there was not even a bed in the house.

"Another pitiable instance of the effects of drunkenness: Catherine Cottier, her two sons, and another youth for trial charged with manslaughter of the keeper of the lodging house with a blow from a flat iron to the head, the whole party being intoxicated.

"John Willis, for causing the death of his wife by pushing her downstairs, both intoxicated.

"William Shaw, an unsophisticated lad only 15 years old, a farm servant at Winwick, sentenced to seven days for stealing two beer glasses at Warrington from the house into which he had been [sic] ticed, as he says, by a fellow servant, and got drunk."

Then followed several more instances including that of a man charged with "rape upon his own daughter, 20 years of age, when inflamed by drink," before Appleton moved on to conditions in the gaol.

"We have been very much crowded of late, but that inconvenience will soon be obviated by the addition, which is in the course of being made, of two new annexes to the cells. With regard to the conduct of the prisoners towards myself and their behaviour during services in chapel, I have not the slightest fault to find. They are very quiet and, in general, apparently most attentive, and although my disappointments and vexations are many, and those of whom I thought I had reason to hope better things frequently return to the gaol, still the good seeds sown are not, I trust, all lost or unproductive, but will be found at the great harvest time to have added some grain, at least, to [be garnered by] the great husbandman of the world."

He remained "my lords and gentlemen, your faithful and obedient servant."

Kirkdale Gaol in 1832. Photo courtesy of Liverpool City Libraries.

Hard drinking; harder living: This is an age when, in the darkness of night, people are either leaving work or going to work. Pieces of burning coal are put out on the pit banking to serve as beacons for the colliers arriving for their shift – for how else would they find their place of employment?

How remote the metropolis must have seemed! In these times, a judge referred to Dartmoor as "one of those large places where criminals are confined in the South of England." A Lancashire leader writer began what looks like an acre or so of small type reflecting his views on Royalty with the words: "We hear very little of Her Majesty, but that little is favourable."

We have the smugness of people secure in their assumed respectability lording it over the less fortunate. In a century when poaching could mean hanging or banishment to Australia and the decimation of families, left to fend for themselves in the absence of a breadwinner, we have a man in court "dressed as a poacher." Now how could that be? Did men dress the part, inviting instant retribution? Did clerks dress as clerks, murderers as murderers?

Here is a male society. You will read little here of women. Wives were there to support the men, and are hardly heard. I began to doubt whether Thomas Grime had a mother until I came across one fleeting reference to her suffering at the time of his conviction. I began to doubt whether he had a wife, until one sentence cropped up confirming that stark fact. What of her feelings? In our own age, women are constantly describing their lives with men who are famous, or infamous. In the 1800s, their views went largely unrecorded and their suffering was their own affair.

It is not an age most people would choose to live in, given choice; but it had the merit of fine language: the beautiful language of the law where people are taken hence and thence, and where sentences run long like rivers in perpetual motion, unhindered by the intrusive stops and commas of modern times. The Elizabethan era alone surpassed it in fine language.

Here, then, the Victorian age; the age of virtuous values, or so we are now reminded by those politicians who would seek to emulate its better parts: an age where people were quick to claim morality but slow to show compassion, and where good and bad died with surprising frequency at an early age; an era of potato blight, cotton famine, the American Civil War, the assassination of Lincoln. And, almost incidentally, the judicial assassination of Thomas Grime, blacksmith, before a carnival crowd gathered to see him go to hell.

How strange it all seems. And how real, even now, when the smell and feel of it are almost tangible through the statements, the denials, the explanations, the directions, and the swift, scratching movements of anonymous pens . . .

Chapter One

"Cruelly I killed Jim Barton"

ONE HUNDRED and more years ago nothing, it seems, so stirred the people and excited them to good humour and the wearing of their best clothes than the prospect of a good public hanging.

A hanging served many purposes. It reminded the populace that crime brought just punishment; it gave evangelists the opportunity to impose their beliefs on others who had little need of them; it broke the monotony of the day; and it rid the world of someone considered, upon judicial inquiry, to be unworthy of remaining in it.

Justice was not always served; but justice, then, as now, is not immaculate: it is necessarily based on what it hears, not what it sees. Since justice has, therefore, the attributes of a blind man with good intent, the limitation does not inevitably lead to the whole truth and nothing but the truth. The law is there to protect as well as to pursue; and on occasion, when it turns its back on a convincing statement because there is no separate evidence to back that statement, it can raise doubts about its precision, although its intentions are good and, no doubt, necessary for the protection of people overall.

It was an age when, if a statement was made to be pored over in court, it was necessary to know, first, the state of sobriety of he who had made it. For in truth, it may well have been an age when, for many, a blurring of the senses was preferable to a sharp realisation of reality.

So, on 1 September, 1866, upwards of 20,000 people, and, by some accounts, 30,000 – fathers, mothers, whole families, the children in "showy" dress – gathered to "see how Tom Grime should die."

Many travelled miles on foot. Others came by excursion train. They were contented and curious: contented because here was a man whose crime had excited "disgust and horror throughout the kingdom"; and curious because the manner of death on a scaffold could never be precisely forecast in advance of the event. The preliminaries to this last macabre dance had the accompaniment of a fiddler in the gathering and a particularly untalented ballad was to be sung about Tom Grime's crime at carnivals:

Cruelly I killed Jim Barton;
Cruelly I did him slay –
Threw his body in a fiery furnace,
And from that place I went away.

Here was the end of a long and morbid affair. Thomas Grime, blacksmith journeyman, aged 30, was dying quickly, with fortitude, and without too much complaint for what had happened three years earlier at Bawk House Pit, known as Button Pit, a small colliery in the township of Haigh, between Chorley and Wigan, in Lancashire, a few hundred yards from Red Rock Bridge, by a canal.

The undisputed facts are that James Barton, father of twelve grown-up children, an engine tenter, or minder, at the pit, was first battered to death or near death, and then fed into his own furnace. The fire burned low and, by a horrifying turn of fate, Barton's son was called upon to re-fire the furnaces. And while the hunt for his father went on, he innocently became the means of completing his cremation.

A plausible motive was to hand, though probably not the correct one; for James Barton, 55, described as "old and inoffensive," possessed a watch which any poor man would covet; a watch easily identifiable, which was proved, subsequently, to have been in the possession of this sentenced man, Thomas Grime. What's more, there was a confession by Grime. Or at least an admission that he was present during the murder. That is why judge, jury and population, in their various ways, though with different degrees of understanding, were well satisfied that Grime was, in September, 1866, properly held at the place from  whence he had come (meaning the confines of a gaol), there to suffer judicial death.

The crowd was well behaved. "Never, we think," wrote a commentator of the time, "has a criminal been launched into eternity for whom so little sympathy was felt."

Thomas Grime was by no means a noble man. He was a known petty criminal, from a poor, working-class Chorley family, with a decent father, who probably despaired of him, and unfortunate friends, with not a great deal to recommend him except the strength he found within himself as his execution approached. He had confessed, had he not? In gaol, he exonerated those he had previously implicated by name in precise terms. He was "wretched" but he was "earnestly preparing himself for eternity."

As a Roman Catholic he turned back to the faith, for there was little help left for him in this world. He had the attentions of a zealous and earnest priest. He was visited by his earliest spiritual counsellor and was reminded of a misspent life. He read religious books. He spoke calmly and with remorse of the disgrace he had brought on his family. He wept "penitently" when visited by relatives. He was, in short, fulfilling the role demanded of him by a moralistic society.

And yet . . . to the end he declared that he never "laid hands on old Barton."

With most people, Grime was reserved and not particularly communicative. To Francis Satterthwaite, scripture reader, and temporary attendant at the prison, he was forthcoming.

"Well, Thomas," said Satterthwaite shortly before the hanging, how are you?"

"Well, owd man," said Grime, "I feel more composed than I have been for some time."

"And do you feel satisfied in your own mind with respect to the affairs?"

"I still maintain," said Grime, "that I never laid hands on the man."

The mob waited patiently, casting an occasional glance at the substantial scaffold whose black drapery moved slightly in a breeze.

"People go to see a man hung as a matter of curiosity, but it is very questionable whether it has the effect of preventing the commission of a single crime or inducing one serious thought," mused a reporter hidden in this great crowd. "The ribald language in which some of the visitors indulged as they proceeded on their way to the scene of the execution was not, at any rate, against the supposition that they were at all affected by the sight they were about to witness."

At 11.55 am, the iron folding doors of the gallows were flung open and a warder known as Tallow Jack appeared. He made some preparation which could not be observed from below.

The crowd expected the bell of the chapel to ring now, but all was silent within the prison. The crowd, too, was hushed. At 12.02 Grime, accompanied by the hangman, William Calcraft, the chaplain and chief warder stood before the crowd. Calcraft was a short, thick-set man (around

5ft 6ins), slightly pockmarked, with a large
mouth, thick lips, and short, black, curly hair. He
was born around 1800 and entered into his office with
these words: "I do hereby most solemnly swear to hang or
behead or otherwise destroy all felons and enemies of our lord the King
and of his subjects duly sentenced according to law and that I will do the
like unto father, mother, sister or brother and all other kindred whatsoever
without favour or hindrance irrespective of sex or age. So help me God."
Grime steadfastly and unflinchingly met the gaze of the thousands in

Calcraft, the hangman

front of him. He was slightly flushed. His lips were seen to move, as if in prayer. This movement could be noted even through a white cap drawn over his head. The chaplain read a psalm in a low voice.

The hangman, in black, and wearing a black cap, placed Grime beneath a massive beam from which a chain a few links long was suspended. He adjusted the rope around Grime's neck and fastened a hook attached to it to the chain above. Hangman and victim then shook hands and the hangman went below. There was a pause of a few seconds, a silence, then a long "Oooh" from the crowd as Grime's body disappeared from sight. There was no observable struggle; just a thud. The last words Grime said were, "Lord Jesus receive my soul."

The carnival was at its end. The hatred, the loathing, the thirst for retribution brought about by a killing horrific by the standards of the time had been satisfied. Thomas Grime was no more.

Such was the emotion of that age that it percolated down well over a century of time. For when a descendant of Grime's family, oblivious of this murder and barely comprehending even the age in which it occurred, stood upon a political platform in Chorley, Grime's town, in the middle of this century as a candidate for local office, someone in the audience, without a word, threw a noose at his feet.

Chapter Two

"A murder most gross, vile, and unnatural"

O N FRIDAY, 2 January 1863, James Barton, fireman and engine tenter, prepared to go on duty at Bawk House Pit, owned by the Earl of Crawford and Balcarres, at Haigh in Lancashire.

The pit had a problem: excessive water. So a pumping engine was kept at work night and day. Three boilers supplied the engine with steam and to each boiler flue there was a separate chimney, all exactly the same height, on the crest of a hill, and seen for miles around. Members of the Barton family shared boiler duties.

The "old" man had fathered twelve children who were grown up, though several still lived in his cottage some two hundred yards from the pit in an area known as "Top Row." "Old" Jim wore a scarf around his neck and a belt around his middle with a small buckle. He was a hard-working man, without a great deal of money; he was apparently respectable and, above all, gainfully employed in an age when money did not come easily. He was not in the habit of taking cash to work (for where would he spend it?), but he did carry a silver watch, easily

The last surviving row of cottages of the three in existence at the time of James Barton.

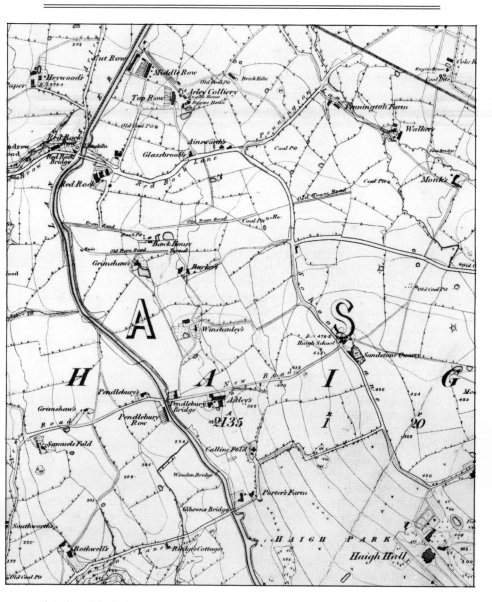

A section of the Ordnance Survey map showing the area around Haigh Hall (bottom right). Bawk House Pit is just to the east of the Leeds & Liverpool Canal, linked to it by a series of tramroads. Top Row is near the top of the map Red Rock and Pendlebury Bridges are clearly visible on the canal.

identified by a number: 17844.

It was around 6 pm. Nothing further was seen or heard of him until 8 pm. He was visited by two workmen – William Wetherby, a platelayer, and William Whalley – who chatted for one hour and ten minutes, then left.

At around 3.15 am, a pit worker (pony tenter) named James Watmough arrived to find the fires virtually out. He looked around for James Barton, but could not find him. This did not perturb him excessively at the time. He sat down to wait and lighted his pipe. Other workmen began to arrive, but still there was no sign of Barton.

The engines were stopped and men needed to be lowered down the pit. Shortly before 5 am a messenger was sent to Barton's son, John (who had to relieve his father at five) informing him of the mystery. Still the old man could not be found. It was at first assumed that he had found some fault in the pumping apparatus and had gone to another works for a man to assist in repairs.

This theory was checked and found to be false. Now minor mystery turned into alarm. Again, a search was made of every conceivable place. Police were told, and arrived between 7 am and 8 am as a fine crisp day was dawning. Nearby ponds were dragged. In improving light, the evidences of violence revealed themselves.

At the entrance to the ash pit beneath the nearest furnace to the pit shaft, cinders were caked in blood. Blood was found, too, on the door of the furnace. There were traces in the boiler house and in a cabin on the nearby pit bank. A crowbar was in the hut.

Ashes from the furnace were put through a sieve. In them: a white substance thought to be half-burned human bones, a few buttons and pieces of buttons, a waist-belt buckle, a couple of teeth, and nails used mainly in boot-making. The placing of the teeth and nails suggested that a body had been thrust into the fire feet foremost.

On a cabin floor nearby were lumps of coal. Was Barton killed – the police wondered – at the door of the cabin as he entered with coal for the cabin fire in his hands? On the wall of the boiler house were finger marks. These and the placing of various objects suggested that Barton might have been alive when he went into the flames – though badly injured at the time.

It was concluded that thieves might have been after that silver watch, which was worth, by various estimates, £5, £9 or £10. There was another conjecture: that the killing might be connected with "a late brutal assault" on a watchman at paper mills half a mile away.

Had Barton been seated with his attackers in his cabin before he went out for the coal, so that they felled him as he re-entered? If that were the case, they were, of course, known to the victim.

Did Barton have some knowledge of the paper mills attack? Was he silenced for that knowledge? There was no immediate answer. At any rate, no trace of the watch was found, and precious little trace of Barton. A small piece of his scarf was on the floor, burned on one side.

So it was murder! Lancashire communities of the time were not accustomed to such violent death. There had been no such happening for all of twenty-five years.

Conjecture had it that, because of the state of the boilers, the time of the murder was around midnight.

People found reports of these events inconceivable. Surely Barton would turn up alive, the victim of some bizarre chain of circumstances so far unrevealed?

"We confess that we, ourselves, had at first great doubt whether the rumours of this revolting case could prove correct," wrote the *Wigan Observer.* "But a close examination of the spot [showed] that the terrible stories conveyed to us were literally correct . . .

"Barton . . . was generally respected; though we have heard numerous whispers against his character, we have found all to have been idle tales, unworthy of belief, and, if true, would not throw any light whatever on the cause of the murder. Of course, the tongue of slanderers have been busy since the sad event, every little scrap which could be [gathered] against the old man serving as the basis of conjecture, generally far from probable, and frequently, utterly ridiculous."

Some twenty-five men were usually employed at the pit and they descended to work around 3.30 each morning. One of Barton's tasks was to take a few burning coals from beneath the boilers to light a fire on the pit bank. This served as a beacon for other workers. The lack of this fire was their first indication that something was wrong.

Watmough had found the fire so nearly out that he did not have sufficient flame for his purpose. It was only by going to the second and third fires that he - with difficulty - got what he required. He thought someone had been firing up the boiler where Barton was incinerated with wood.

Barton's son, helped by a brother, subsequently lit this boiler because steam was needed for the engine and from then until police arrived, he was working normally, believing that his father would turn up. So, in all, the body spent some six to eight hours in the furnace.

On the Monday afternoon, the furnace was cleared of ashes and these were carefully searched. More pieces of bone were found. One buckle was identified as that worn on the murdered man's belt;

another came from his braces.

Police, meanwhile, were interested in the watch and made a careful note of its detail. Made by Robert Croskell, of Liverpool; a silver patent lever, roughly (known as "russet") finished, with second hand, attached to a steel chain with long links, with key and steel seal. Barton also had a pocket knife and tobacco box. Neither could be found.

Had the watch gone into the furnace with him? This theory was discounted, because although it might melt, traces would be left.

Observers drew curious parallels between old Barton's death and that of a man named Coulton 25 years earlier, the district's last previous homicide. Coulton had been shot. Barton worked under his supervision at the time. It was supposed that more than one person was involved in this latest murder because it would require great strength to lift a man and throw him through a fire hole in the face of intense heat.

Soon after the murder, a meeting of the county magistrates in the borough of Wigan heard that the Earl of Crawford was offering a reward of £200 for the apprehension and conviction of "the perpetrators of the murder most gross, vile and unnatural."

A notice was posted the same evening:

THERE WAS MURDER – £200 REWARD.

Whereas in the night time between 9 on Friday the 2nd and 3 on Saturday the 3rd, 1863, James Barton, of 55 years, colliery engine man in the employment of the Right Honourable the Earl of Crawford and Balcarres, at Bawk House, Old Button Pit, near Red Rock Bridge, Haigh, near Wigan, was, whilst on his duty, vilely murdered by some person or persons not known and his body was burnt in the furnace: A reward of £200 will be paid to any person who may give such information as shall lead to the apprehension and conviction of the murderer/murderers. Information to be given to the Chief Constable of Lancashire Constabulary at Preston, to Chief Superintendent Ellison, or Inspector Peters, at Pemberton or Hindley.

– Mayhew and Sons, solicitors to the said Earl, of Wigan. January 5th, 1863.

Rumour confounded rumour as gossip gathered strength. Tramps were known to pass the night in cabins erected on pit banks. Could a tramp have killed Barton because he was enforcing an order that they were not allowed to rest there?

A lunatic had escaped from a workhouse during a recent fearful storm. He had since been recaptured – but could he have had a hand in the murder?

How strong was the connection, if any, between events at the pit and the paper mill?

Shortly before noon on the Tuesday, a coroner's jury was assembled two miles from the pit, but the hearing was adjourned. Police were reluctant to reveal all they knew, or surmised. They also wished to delay a burial of the remains while they might offer some further clues.

Meanwhile, news of the scandalous destruction of old Barton had reached London and the Secretary of State for the Home Department added £100 to the reward money offered by the Earl of Crawford. He also stated "that he would advise Her Majesty [Victoria] to pardon any accomplice who did not actually commit the crime if he gave the required information."

It was a considerable sum of money for the time, and it might well have produced more false information than truth (noted later in this account). But for the time being, the *Wigan Observer* sadly stated:

"We have nothing to add to the very full report which we published last week of this horrible atrocity. It was hoped that the offer of the handsome reward . . . coupled with a free pardon . . . might have had the effect of inducing a confession. We regret that this has not been the case. We are afraid that the chances of the capture of the criminals now daily grow less and less, especially as the county police, who have been hard at work since the murder, have not obtained any information which is likely to lead to the conviction of any of the suspected persons . . . The pit was visited Sunday last by hundreds anxious to inspect the cabin, with a struggle for a place to peep into the furnace where Barton's body was thrust, and to draw their own conclusions as to the manner in which the murder was perpetrated and the body disposed of."

The delayed inquest finally took place at the home of a Mr F. Hall, of New Springs, near Wigan before Mr C. Driffield, coroner, and the jurors who had been so swiftly dispensed with initially. A small coffin containing the few reminders of Barton's existence was placed on a table.

The first witness was Watmough, the pony tenter of the pit. He had last seen Barton around 6 pm on Friday, the second, as he left work. "The following morning, I reached the pit shortly after 3 am. I found the pumping engine stopped. The cabin fire was nearly out and lumps of coal were lying on the floor of the cabin. Not finding Barton, I went into the boiler house and shouted, but received no reply. I returned to the cabin and in doing so, noticed Barton's muffler lying half burned. I sat down for two or three minutes, then the fireman, Matthew Rhoden came. I said to him: 'See yo here – part of old Jim's muffler, burnt.' We wondered where Barton had gone, then began to look for him, but found nothing. About 4.30, I went to the boiler for a spadeful of fire with which to put a light at the pit brow [hill]. The door of the first furnace was latched. I opened it with a spade. There was very little fire. It looked quite dead, as though [it] had been fired with wood all night. There might, perhaps, be a shovelful of fire on each side, but in the middle, it was quite white. The white looked like burnt wood.

"I told Rhoden I could not get any fire there, so he held a light for me to go to the second. This furnace seemed to have been baked. I got the fire from there and took it to the brow [then] I went to the house of [Barton's] son, John, who sent me to his father's house to see whether he had gone home. Then he went to the colliery."

The son who had unwittingly assisted in the cremation of his own father gave his evidence. He had found the engine stopped and fired all three fire-holes so as to get up steam as quickly as possible, and saw nothing to alarm him in the process. As light came, he saw the evidence of struggle: finger marks on the walls; the crowbar which appeared to him to have traces of blood. From the state in which he found the fires, he concluded they had been unattended for some three to four hours. It was always the practice to fire up with slack or coal, never with timber.

Both friends and strangers, he said, were in the habit of calling at the cabin to smoke a pipe . . . "I spent most of the time in the cabin. We first thought that my father was in the furnace from the discovery of blood upon the plate against which the furnace door was shut." No, he did not know of anyone against whom his father had a grudge. The older man was on good terms with others at the colliery. Nor could he think of a reason why his life should be taken – except for the watch, now missing. "I have never heard my father say that he knew anything about men who attacked the watchman at Standish Paper Mills." The old man was not, in fact, on duty on that night: the son was.

George Armstrong, of Blackrod, foreman, reached the pit at around 4.30 am and found what looked like blood on the door of the furnace. "It looked like stuff that had run out of a pie in an oven." Cakes of blood were found beneath the fire.

From all this, and more, the coroner concluded, not unnaturally, that the remains were those of a human and that a man was missing. There had been mention of a crowbar with spots upon it which were supposed to be blood but which, during tests, were found not to be blood.

The jury came to the desired conclusion: that James Barton was wilfully murdered by some person or persons, who placed him in the fire where his remains were found. They had been considering the matter for five hours.

Shortly after this hearing there was great commotion in Wigan when it was rumoured that police had a man in custody who had admitted knowing something of the murder and the murderers.

A drunk, in a public house named the Windsor Castle, had provided unlikely information and was arrested for his pains. He was locked up and duly appeared before two magistrates. A large crowd gathered in court, and before them appeared a man aged between forty and fifty, who had formerly given his name as Lamberton, from Coppull, but who now gave it as William Hawkinson; and he was wearing dress "common to poachers."

A Sgt Whalley gave his account of the matter. He had been opposite the Windsor Castle when he saw a crowd. In the kitchen of the public house he found some fifty people standing around a drunken man who said "there were seven of them who had to do with the murder," and that as one of them found that Barton knew them, they set to and put him in the furnace. Hawkinson said he knew all seven men.

It then emerged that he had made previous similar statements "and had given the names of persons. But upon inquiry it was found not to be true."

Sober, the prisoner was less than helpful. "I have nothing to say," he declared. If he had anything to say previously it was because he was drunk and certainly more than he knew. The police understood he was a colliery worker from Adlington, but was so often drinking that he could not get to work.

So with a fine of five shillings for drunkenness, the magistrates dispensed with him.

Chapter Three

Coal and The Famine

T HERE is now a lull in affairs, where those who knew did not speak, and those who spoke did not know: in short, a period of total bafflement in which police exhausted their theories, and people their imaginations. A considerable time passed before the excitements of 1863 were renewed. We can usefully pause, here, and examine the conditions and practices of the age.

The community of Haigh was overshadowed by Wigan in whatever it did, and Wigan, with its Celtic and Roman background, stood for mines and mining. It was among the first ten townships of England to receive its borough charter (in the first year of the reign of Henry 1, AD 1100). Here, in this town, seven times plundered during the Civil War on account of its loyalty to King Charles, large numbers of people lived in appalling conditions and worked in darkness.

The state of affairs in the 1840s is uniquely summed up in the words of an eight-year-old girl. She was a trapper: that is, she sat in a hole, near the door, at the pit bottom, opening and shutting it by means of a piece of string. This was part of the business of ventilating the mine. Those who performed the work were usually between the ages of five and eight.

"I have to trap without a light," she said, "and I'm scared. I go at four, and sometimes half past three, in a morning and come out at five and half past in the evening. I never go to sleep. Sometimes I sing when I've light, but not in the dark. I dare not sing then."

The only light came when some pitman gave her a small piece of candle. Working twelve to eighteen hours a day, children earned 2s 6d to 3s a week.

Fillers loaded tubs and skips after men had hewn the coal. Pushers, or hurriers, pushed the tubs from the coal face to the foot of the shaft. There was an alternative to pushers in some pits – "a girdle is put round the naked waist, to which a chain from the carriage is hooked

and passed between the legs, and boys crawl on their hands and knees, drawing the carriage after them."

In 1842 the *First Report of the Commission on Children and Young Persons* contained this description of girl pushers at work: "Chained, belted, harnessed like dogs in a go-cart, black, saturated with wet, and more than half-naked, crawling upon their hands and feet and dragging heavy loads behind them, they present an appearance indescribably disgusting and unnatural."

That report also told of men and women, completely naked, working side by side. Some women gave birth underground. A witness told the commissioners, "I have worked in a pit since I was six years old. I have four children, two born while I worked in the pit. I had a child born in the pits and I brought it up the pit shaft in my skirt."

There was disease and deformity. Women fought like men and swore like men.

Miners' cottages were "hovels rather than cottages, having nothing but a ground floor. Some consist of only one, others of two rooms, from ten to fourteen feet square each. Many of the older ones have no ceiling; vacancies in the roof let in wind and rain; the floor is damp, being often little more than the natural ground."

"The collier, black from head to foot [generally] sits down on a stool in front of the fire and washes face, neck, breast, arms, shoulders, and legs to the knees – often not so far. He washes his head on Saturdays. The rest of his person remains untouched by water."

Improvements came slowly. A former miner, speaking of conditions in Wigan around 1910, said, "In some of these back-to-back houses there was only one room up and one room down. They had no gas and used to have to burn an oil lamp or candles."

In some pits, it was normal to let down a lighted candle to discharge gas. Explosions of firedamp were a constant hazard. The commission of 1842 reported of one pit near Haigh that children worked from 5 am to 6 pm in entire darkness, as candles could not be afforded. Most had been workhouse apprentices.

Few areas of the county were better provided with accessible coal seams and few have been more extensively worked over the centuries. The Wigan coalfield took in around seventy square miles and Haigh, noted for cannel (a gas-producing fuel with the appearance of black marble, clean to the touch and capable of being intricately carved), had a prominent role.

In 1863, its miners were raising 400,000 tons of coal annually. The great Haigh Sough (begun, 1652, completed 1670) had been one of the great wonders of its age. This sough (pronounced as in rough), or tunnel, ventilated by ten vertical shafts, was constructed to enable the cannel coal under Haigh to be worked "without fear of inundation" from various old workings full of water. It was two-thirds of a mile long, four feet high, six feet wide and drained into the River Douglas by way of a brook.

The cannel seams were, in general, three feet thick and supplies were distributed by canal to such places as Preston and the north, Blackburn, Manchester and Liverpool.

One Sir Roger Bradshaigh was landowner at the time of the great sough, and his orders to workers were many and peremptory: "Any hewer or getter who does not send up cannel in large lumps, as convenient for the basket or sledge, shall, for each offence, be fined 3d, and for every several default afterwards, 6d, half to Roger Bradshaigh and half to the informer." To ensure that a full day's work was given, fines were to be applied where the hewers sent up less than thirty full baskets per day, or twenty on Saturdays.

A map of 1796, by James Leigh, described Haigh as Lane Ends, and detailed some remarkable names:

> Nearer Priest Hey, Further Bears Acre, Field at back o'th House, Elles Acre, Great Marled Earth, Sour Field, Heifer's Croft, Sweet Grass, Higher Tagg, Further Butter Scholes, Nearer Butter Scholes, Long Shoot, Black Earth, Red Earth, Hard Field.

The village then consisted of few buildings, although there was an ironworks, begun in 1790, which was to produce the first locomotive used in Lancashire (it carried coal). Between that map and the ordnance survey of 1840 Haigh had acquired St David's Church, a brewery, a school building, a smithy and two pubs: the Balcarres Arms and Red Lion; but it was still Lane Ends.

For those in employment in mid-century, the railways were broadening horizons. Here, the words of the government inspector sent to Blackpool in 1849 to report on whether, under the Public Health Act of 1848, the town justified a democratically elected Board of Health to administer its affairs: "The labouring classes generally live in small villages and detached cottages in the neighbourhood. Owing to this circumstance, few of those scenes of extreme filth and wretched accommodation which mark the purlieus of most places, are to be met with, and I may characterise Blackpool as being in a particularly clean state if it is compared with its sister towns in Lancashire. This state of cleanliness will, unfortunately, be seen to be only comparative."

The inspector, Benjamin Herschel Babbage, would note that many lodging houses kept livestock in their own backyards; that in a town of 421 houses there were 181 pigsties but only 112 water closets; that the average age at death was a mere twenty-five, and this, you will note, in "a health resort."

Lancashire and Yorkshire Railway posters advertised "Sea bathing for the working classes" and offered people in Grime's home town of Chorley day excursions to Fleetwood and Blackpool at 2s (10p) for males and 1s for females and children.

Providing the next meal is more likely to have been the immediate concern of these same "working classes." And poaching – as we shall see later – could have been a factor in the death of James Barton.

Nowadays, poaching is, to a degree, a sport: a contest between hunter and gamekeeper. Or, if it becomes a trade, it is done on a scale sufficiently large to merit the effort. Few, in Britain today, could claim that they poach out of urgent necessity.

But poaching was certainly a necessity for many in the nineteenth century, and particularly in those years before Victoria came to the throne in 1837. Between 1827 and 1830 more than 8,500 men were convicted under the Game Laws. Some were hanged, some shipped to Australia. It was only in the middle of the century, when distress – nationally – was not so great, and laws were less severe, that poaching diminished.

In 1865, when a Lancashire landowner – Henry Petre, of Dunkenhalgh, near Accrington – granted his tenants the privilege of killing game on their land, he was given an illuminated address.

When the loss of a rabbit might mean the loss of a man, families, villages were decimated and the Game Laws caused great wretchedness. Poor families were often on the verge of starvation. They could look with sympathy to Ireland where potato disease ruined the crop and brought starvation there.

This is an age of which one man could write: "I could tell you of mothers dividing a farthing herring and a halfpennyworth of potatoes among a family of seven."

In the year James Barton died, there was a cotton famine brought about by the American Civil War. The distress lasted from the latter end of 1861 to the early months of 1865. Soup kitchens opened everywhere. The Riot Act was read at Blackburn in East Lancashire – not all that far from Haigh, and a mere nine miles from the place where the man who died for his murder lived.

Special constables were sworn in. A troop of Lancers was sent.

By the end of 1862 hundreds of thousands of people in Lancashire were in want of food. The pawn shops were overflowing with their possessions, and 25 to 47 per cent of populations of whole manufacturing districts were receiving relief. It is estimated that more than 420,000 people were engaged in the textile trade at that time, every one affected by shortage of cotton. Shopkeepers were ruined in every town and village. A Mansion House fund raised more than £500,000; a committee of Lancashire noblemen and MPs raised £52,000. The loss of wages was at the rate of £136,094 a week.

Such was the world in which the miners of Haigh followed the flaring of coals in the night.

Such was the world of James Barton, labelled "old man" at the age of 55, and dead in his own furnace. . .

Chapter Four

A confession from afar

I N OCTOBER, 1865, came what appeared to be the first real breakthrough in the investigation into the murder of James Barton. A prisoner at Warwick Gaol had made a confession.

John Healey (alias Donnelly, alias McDermott), aged 22, of Haigh, was that man. He was in custody for burglary and was taken to Wigan and charged with murder: a young vagrant of light complexion and shambling gait who appeared far from robust. This, according to evidence of the time, was his story, given to John Mills Anderson, governor of the gaol:

"I have something particular to tell you, and until I do so, I can not rest at night without being troubled by my dreams.

"I was concerned in the Wigan outrage about 18 months ago. I was, at that time, on tramp. I met with four others in a public house near Wigan. We had some whisky together. They made me go with them to the engine house where Barton was. He was sitting there. We robbed him of his watch and money and then we put him in the fire. I was obliged to do it in self defence, or they would have done something terrible to me and I was afraid of them. I did not put him in the fire. I held his legs while they put him in. We all fled. I don't know what became of the others. I got nothing for it but some whisky and I've been miserable ever since."

A police superintendent named Ellison, who had travelled to Warwick from Wigan to see the prisoner, asked him "where he had come from on the day of the murder" and he said:

"I walked from Liverpool to Chorley and left Chorley again the same night about 6 o'clock. I walked an hour or an hour-and-a-half in the direction of Wigan. I was benighted and sat down on the roadside about a mile from the place. I was drunk. How long I had been there, I can't tell you, when four men came up and asked me where I was going. I said, 'Nowhere in particular'. They began to talk to me and press me to go with them, but being a stranger, I was afraid."

They drank whisky together in a public house, from a bottle one of the other men already had in his pocket, then: "We all went to the engine boilerhouse where [Barton] was shovelling coals. One of the four men got hold of Barton by the neck and gave him a blow with his fist, knocking him down, and took out his watch and money. We then got him in the fireplace. Barton kicked and struggled very much while the men were putting him in the fire. I do not know whether the engine was going when we went into the boilerhouse.

"The four men were very tall, dressed in fustian jackets. They had caps on, and were drunk. After we had done it, we went in the direction of Wigan and I went in the day to Ashton in the Willows to look for work."

The man was remanded into custody.

When he next appeared before magistrates, both his appearance ("far worse than when he first came") and his story had changed. He looked indifferent during his examination and his voice was almost inaudible as he declined to question witnesses. The court was not full, which suggested that news of the man's further examination had not spread around town.

One magistrate was Jonathan Lamb. This interchange took place between him and the prisoner Healey:

"Is what you stated [to the goal governor] correct?"

"It is not all correct, sir. I own to it that I had liquor with them, but then I do not recollect after where I went."

"That portion about the murder?"

"I can remember meeting the men and afterwards getting drunk, but I do not know what occurred after that."

"You do not recollect what took place after you had the drink with these men?"

"No."

"Well, then, how was it you made the statement?"

"A man may be in drink and does not know what he is doing."

"Yes, but you were not in drink when you made the statement."

"No."

"Well, what made you make the statement?"

There was no reply from Healey.

Next came various witnesses to the events of January, 1863, who repeated what was generally known of Barton's killing. Barton's son, on this occasion, noted that the furnaces were "eight feet long, four feet wide and the doors 16 inches square."

There was evidence from a boat worker, who recalled the night of the murder: "I was working close to the canal bank, knocking full tubs of coal off a boat. The towing path is on the opposite side of the canal to the colliery. There is a light at the colliery which lights the path, and it was moonlight also.

"At about quarter to two in the morning, I saw four men coming along the tow path from Haigh way. They were walking sharply. Their jackets were buttoned up and their collars were turned up. They went quickly past, then stopped the other side of the bridge. I shouted to [another worker] that there were some men."

The prisoner was then committed to trial at the next Assizes charged "on your own confession with having, on the night of the 2nd or morning of the 3rd January, 1863, at Haigh in this county, wilfully and of your own malice and aforethought murdered one James Barton at the Bawk House Colliery of Haigh." He was taken to Kirkdale Gaol in Liverpool.

The distance from pit to road was around a quarter of a mile. The road was close to the canal.

Now all this sounds convincing enough 125 years after the event, but the *Wigan Observer* of the time did not find it so.

"Few if any," it declared, "accept the confession as true, whilst the majority are strongly of the opinion that the story has been entirely fabricated. The police, in particular, are very decidedly of the opinion that no credence is to be attached to the tale of Healey, who they scarcely know whether to regard more as a knave or fool.

"From Mr Superintendent Ellison's evidence, it will be seen that he was in possession of the facts as long ago as April last and we believe that he was so convinced of the untruthfulness of the prisoner's words that he did not deem it necessary to take any steps in the matter.

"He was taken by surprise when Mr Healey was apprehended on the charge. Indeed, we have been informed, but we do not vouch for the fact, that there is evidence to show that the fellow was actually in Preston on the night of the murder, and should this be the case, of course, all belief in the story must be at an end.

"Independently, however, of this, it is in the highest degree improbable that a party of men on the way to commit a murder, or even robbery only, would ask a stranger to accompany them. It is also improbable that one man should have consented to help a lot of persons he did not know to commit so horrible a deed.

"Then, Healey said [the party] were drinking whisky at a public house in Wigan on the night of the murder. It is not believed possible [sic] that five tramps could have been drinking in any tavern, either in or near Wigan that night, without it having come to the knowledge of the police.

"The confession says that Barton, the murdered man, was in the engine house at the pit shovelling coals when the five men reached this place, but the circumstantial evidence strongly contradicts this. There is little doubt that, when attacked, he was seated, as was his custom, in a little cabin on the pit bank [for] there were signs that a severe struggle had taken place therein. The seat was spotted with blood. Blood was found [sic] on a crow bar lying on the floor, and the outside wall of the cabin at the side nearest to the firehole was also besprinkled. If the prisoner has told the truth about the party drinking whisky together at a public house, he will surely be able to point out the place, and then he might be corroborated in a very important particular.

"So far as can be presently judged, he is quite unable to do this; and besides, he can say nothing about the neighbourhood of the pit which gives the idea that he was present when the crime was committed. An opinion gaining ground [is] that the story has been invented by the prisoner in the hope that he will be able thus to induce the authorities at Warwick Gaol, by whom he was treated with all the strictness prescribed for a frequently convicted criminal, to relax the regulations or transfer him at once to Lancashire for trial on the graver charge.

"When a remark of his fate was made in his presence on Saturday, he all but admitted such was the fact."

The newspaper conceded, however, that there were those who believed Healey's first statement – "it was not made public at the time that four men acting very suspiciously were seen walking along the canal from the direction of Bawk House Pit shortly after two o' clock on the morning of the murder. This evidence, therefore, must be considered as corroborative of a confession."

Chapter Five

The missing watch

THE (by now) thoroughly bewildered citizens of Lancaashire had barely digested this 'confession' when they were confronted by another. In the following month – November 1865 – it was being hinted that the police were keeping to themselves a statement "which has upon it much greater marks of probability than the one made by Healey".

In custody was a man named Thomas Walton, "known" to the police as a shifty character, and notable for the fact that one of his legs was shorter than the other. He was commonly called Steppy or Stepper and had no settled address, but was in the habit of roaming canal banks and living in coal pit cabins. His eyes were sunken; he had what was mysteriously described as "a hanging forehead"; and those who observed him concluded that his mental capacity was not all that high. The "hanging forehead" was obviously deceptive. Walton was to prove far more intelligent than he appeared.

This man was drinking in a canal-side beer house when he mentioned to the landlord that he was an accomplice in the murder of James Barton. The landlord informed the police and the man was put in the dock at Wigan on a capital charge.

The ale house, it would appear, was the confessional box of the time and the landlord, Alexander Shepherd, described the homely conversation that took place before he obligingly informed the police.

"I was sitting down, and he came to me and said, 'Alex, they suspect that I am one of the murderers of Barton's job.' I said, 'How can that be?' He said, 'I do not know, but they do.' Then he said, 'I did not strike the blow myself, nor did I put him into the fire. When I was in the cabin there were three of us, and Barton came up with two pieces of coal which he was carrying in his hand. One of the men struck him, but Barton caught the first blow to save himself. Barton asked one of the other men, 'Will you stand for this?' They struck him twice more and took him and shoved him into the fire. I opened the firehole while they put him in . . . Healey was not there when they threw the watch in . . ."

The landlord was well aware of the murdered man's missing silver watch, so he said, "Into where?" and Walton replied, "Into the canal."

"I asked whereabouts, and he said, 'Near to Pendlebury's Bridge between George Bridge and Pendlebury Bridge.' I asked if it was near the road and he said, 'No, near the corner just past the road'."

Next, another reminder of the curious social relationships of the time. A policeman walked into the pub. The landlord said, "I was just thinking about you," and the policeman replied, "What's the matter?"

"Well," said the landlord, "here is a man confessing about Barton's murder." The policeman took Walton into another room and Walton repeated his story. The policeman slowly wrote it down, then announced that he was obliged to go away "to some rough company at New Springs"; a pub, apparently, because he intended to turn this rough company out. As a matter of convenience he left his prisoner in the custody of the landlord, who asked whether he should have any beer. The policeman saw no harm in his having a pint.

Walton must have been in a highly talkative mood because he then described a robbery at the paper mill close by the pit where Barton died. He said "they" beat the watchman. "I was the man that pulled the drawer out but there was nothing in it. The watchman sat dozing. [Then] he woke up and asked us what we were doing there. We said we would give him, 'What were we doing there?' and thrashed him."

When the policeman returned, Walton obligingly repeated that story, too.

In court, the landlord was asked whether Walton was drunk or sober when he told his story. "He was fresh in drink," said the landlord, and not quite sober, but he appeared to know what he was saying.

The prisoner, by this time, could "not recollect anything of the sort."

He said, "I do not know whether it is true or a lie. I have no knowledge of it, and I do not recollect seeing the policeman, but I do remember seeing him [the witness] during the day when I was drinking there."

The landlord: "He never saw me during the day. It was at night."

Walton: "I was told he was offering me 20 sovereigns to tell him about this affair at the Bawk House. It is a great lie if I said so. I have no knowledge of the affair at all. None whatsoever."

The morning after his arrest, Walton was back at the landlord's pub, (between 6 am and 7 am) declaring, "I am not worth having, you see, so they sent me back".

"I was surprised," said the landlord. "I slipped down to the policeman [presumably his house], called to him, and asked him how it was that this man had come back. He spoke to me through the room window. He said the sergeant would not have him and he took him home."

The landlord was asked, "When he came the following morning, was he quite sober?"

"Yes."

"Did you tell him what he had said the night before?"

"Yes."

"What did he say?"

"He said he knew what he had said. When parties asked him what he had said, he replied, 'The policeman knows what I have said and he had it down'."

"Did he say whether it was true or not?"

"He did not say which it was. We blamed him for not apologising, or regretting, but he did neither."

The prisoner: "I could not apologise for a thing I knew nothing about. I had three pints paid for me when I came in first thing in the morning."

Shepherd the landlord declared: "I said the policeman had taken you up on suspicion of murder and the next moment you came in."

The prisoner: "There is not a word of truth in it. If I had said that, I must have been dreaming the words and catching them whilst I was asleep . . . I do not know anything about the affair except what I saw in the papers and what conjecture and supposition there has been all through." Then, turning to the landlord, "Alex, I think you have made a little bit of this . . ."

When laughter in court had subsided, Walton said, "I should be very sorry to tell you a thing like that to raise confusion throughout the country and especially with regard to the relatives of the deceased."

PC Elias Worthington spoke of questioning the prisoner at the beer house run by Alexander Shepherd. This is his account:

"I asked him, 'What is this you have been talking about Barton's murder?' He said, 'I know all about it.' He said, 'Who committed the robbery and assault at Standish Paper Mill in December, 1862?', and I said I knew nothing about it. He continued, 'I do. The watchman was sleeping in one corner of the room. I opened the drawer and found no money. The watchman woke up and said, 'What are you doing here?' I said, 'Seize him' and one of the parties [present] then struck the watchman with the stave of a barrow. The night Barton was murdered, a party of us were drinking at a beer house called Dychers in Wigan

Lane. We were drinking up to shutting [closing] time and then we brought more beer away with us and sat down in a lane together. During the time we were drinking, a man came in the direction of Chorley and I said, 'Where are you going?' He said he did not know – anywhere. I asked him to drink and he sat down and drank for some time. [Then] we gave him some whisky out of a pop bottle. After we had been drinking some time we went to the Bawk House Pit and found Barton, with two lumps of coal in his hands. Barton said to one of the men, 'You will see me put on?' and he replied, 'I will, for you have been telling tales.' [Barton said], 'I have not.' He was put on: I opened the door whilst the other parties put him into the furnace. Barton was not murdered for the sake of his watch and money, but more for revenge of one of them suspecting him [of] telling tales to the [game]keepers. They murdered him for that.'

The policemen then "asked the prisoner, 'Who were the men?' and he replied, 'I dare not tell. I saw one of the parties two years ago in Runcorn [Cheshire]. He asked me what news there was, and told me if I said anything about it I would be shot.' The prisoner then mentioned the name of the man who knocked Barton down with a lump of iron, and continued, 'There was a scuffle afterwards. When we came away we brought the watch with us. The man to whom Barton spoke remarked on the canal bank that Barton was done with, and they must make away with the watch. The watch was chucked into the canal near Pendlebury Row'."

The policeman concluded that the prisoner was not sober, but he repeated his words on their second meeting the same night and the two of them were at the beer house until "near one o'clock in the morning," in which time no further drink had been taken.

The policeman had spoken to the prisoner for all of one and three quarter hours in all, and yet now the prisoner was declaring that he could not remember seeing him at all.

Walton, taken into custody by the constable, released on the direction of a superior office, had then been taken in charge by a Sgt Gardener of Wigan division.

Gardener asked the man what he had been saying about the murder of Barton and he replied, "I only said about two words in Alec Shepherd's beer house, and this officer and Alec were trying to make a deal more of it." The sergeant was sceptical – "You said above two words." Walton replied, "I only said there was a man in Kirkdale [Gaol] who has confessed." The sergeant told him that if that were the case, the man was invisible; and as he locked up Walton, the prisoner said, "I am taking my last journey. I shall be hanged for this."

Now came a different story altogether from Walton:
"I was with [a man named] Evan Kershaw with a boat at the top lock at Aspull, and I was lying on the floor all night. There was another man in the boat called Tom Bowling. I remember that night very well, for Bowling had a watch in the cabin. He wakened in the night and asked me what time it was. I said I did not know and he told me to look at his watch, which was hanging up. I did look and it was ten minutes past two. I helped a bit at the locks near Rose Bridge and he gave me a shilling for my trouble. I never went near the Bawk House Pit until the Saturday. I went there in the afternoon."

Prisoner: "No, a Sunday."

Sgt Gardener: "He told me, 'on a Saturday'." He added that the prisoner was drunk when he spoke to him, though "not very drunk. He walked from New Springs to Hindley with me."

The prisoner was remanded to Kirkdale Gaol, and, amid growing confusion about the truth of all these confessions, inquiries continued.

Chapter Six

Walton is charged

THOMAS WALTON, alias Steppy, charged on his own confession with being concerned with the murder of James Barton at Button Pit, again appeared before magistrates on November 30, 1865, but police were not ready to proceed, and information was given only in private. A week-end intervened before Walton again appeared. The court was crowded.

Thomas Bowling, now employed in a Chorley factory, but previously a canal boatman, added his own account to Walton's description of his night in a boat at the time of Barton's murder.

"I recollect the time James Barton was murdered. I heard about it, but was boating at the time. The prisoner was in the habit of sleeping in our boat when he was not working. The nearest I can think, it was between 10 and 11 when Evan Kershaw [the owner of the boat] and Walton came into the boat. I was there. They were both very drunk and laid down. Evan went to bed and Walton lay on the cabin floor. The prisoner got up towards the morning and asked what time it was and I said, 'Half past two'. He then went to the table and Evan said, 'Look to see if Steppy [Walton's nickname] takes your watch with him.' I do not know what time of year it was when he slept in the cabin, but I know it was winter."

A statement made by Walton to police and recalled by an Inspector Peters, of Hindley (near Wigan) Police, declared: "On the night of the murder I slept with three men named Thomas Bowling, William Hodgkinson and William Kershaw. Hodgkinson is now in Preston Gaol. I slept in Evan Kershaw's boat cabin at Top Lock. Three days before Barton's murder I had been drinking at Alec Shepherd's beer house, and on the night of Barton's murder the three men above mentioned left with me and went to the boat cabin and went to sleep until morning; and in the morning we heard of Barton's murder and went to the place. I do not recollect who went with me. I had been drinking for a week. I do not remember seeing the policeman [in the pub where Walton was arrested]. I have not, to my knowledge said those words in that paper [the statement implicating him]. There is not a single word of truth in it."

The hearing was adjourned and re-convened two days later before the same magistrates. Again, the court was crowded. Through questioning, Walton was careful to point out that no witness called had seen him at the pit around the time of the murder.

"Did *you* see me there, John?" he asked the son of the murdered man (a question he had put to other witnesses).

Answer: "No."

"How long is it that you saw me about the colliery previous to this taking place?"

"Three years."

The clerk: "The murder took place in January, 1863. Was it three years before that?"

John Barton: "Yes, three or four years previously."

Walton was told he would be committed for trial at Liverpool Assizes accused of murder, and made this statement:

"On the night that Barton was murdered, I was not within two miles of the place, and I have had no complicity in it, not the least, and there is no person who can prove I have. On Monday, 5 January, near the colliery, I bought a special Wigan paper giving a description of the murder and how the murder was supposed to have been committed. I know nothing about it, only what I have read and heard. That is all."

He was then removed to Kirkdale Gaol.

Chapter Seven

The canal is dredged

ON TUESDAY 19th December, 1865, John Healey, 22, and Thomas Walton, 33, were charged, at Liverpool Assizes, on their own separate confessions, with the murder of James Barton.

"How say you" – Healey was asked – "Guilty or Not Guilty?"

"Guilty," he replied.

"Do you mean that you wilfully and with malice aforethought took part in the murder of this man?"

"I am as guilty as a child unborn before baptism."

"You mean you are not guilty?"

There was no answer.

"Do you desire the officer to enter a plea of not guilty?"

"Yes."

Walton also pleaded not guilty.

Mr Aspinall, QC, for the prosecution, then addressed himself to the vexed question of the murdered man's silver watch. If, indeed, it had been thrown into the canal, should the canal not be dredged for the evidence? It was a practical proposition, though not an easy task. Expense would be high. It would be time consuming. Considerable traffic would be interfered with. And there was the question of time lapse making the search more difficult.

He told the judge it would not be easy to empty the canal at the point indicated because there was a long space between locks.

The judge remarked, not unreasonably, "It strikes me there has been some neglect on the part of those who have known of these matters so long that they have not [dredged] before." Mr Aspinall pointed out that Healey had been committed only the previous month.

The trial was then postponed so that a search could be made. It involved interference with a long stretch of water and a high degree of embarrassment as we learn from the *Wigan Observer*'s account. On 9

March, the newspaper reported:

"Since [postponement of the trial] police have used every exertion to make the necessary arrangements for the examination. The canal company have not, until the present time, shown any disposition to allow the running off of the water which was necessary, the first, and indeed the principal, objection which was alleged stood in the way being the scarcity of water at the Yorkshire end of the canal. A few days ago, however, the requisite permission was granted for the inspection to be made last Sunday, and the most extensive preparations were made to ensure thorough overhaul of the mud to lie very thickly beneath the water."

Dams were formed at two points and "water was then drawn off by a 16-inch pipe to a point close to the pit [where the murder took place]. It was expected that by two in the morning the canal would be clear. At 11, however, when only some two feet of water remained to be drawn off, an accident happened which completely destroyed all the calculations and inflicted considerable disappointment to all concerned in the task; for the dam at Red Rock Bridge end proved faulty in construction and was inadequate to resist the water lying against it. An unusual blubbing was noticed, and workmen on the [dam] platform had just time to reach the side, when the water lashed through with a force so great as to fill a thousand yards in a little more than ten minutes. At this time, there was great confusion, and beyond the stoppage of the outflow, nothing could be done to lessen the disaster."

Disaster it certainly was, for 115 navvies from the water works and 35 boatmen and others employed on the canal were ready, waiting to examine the mud. There was also a sturdy contingent from the law: a small army of constables together with their leaders. They were watched with interest by a vast number of the populace glad of the entertainment. The canal men who erected the dams were "unmercifully chafed." The operation was postponed for a week.

At the second attempt "every preparation was made to guard against accident," and the workmen employed by the canal company certainly improved considerably on their first efforts.

Sheeting to form a dam was fixed at Gibson's Bridge and at Arley Bridge nearly a mile beyond Button Pit. This time, the barriers were of sufficient strength, and at 4.20 pm the process of running off water was begun at Arley Bridge and near Red Rock Bridge. The distance between the two dams was almost one and three quarter miles and the water emptied into a brook was estimated at 760,000 cubic feet.

Workmen reaching the spot early on Sunday morning nevertheless

found that two feet of water were still lying between Gibson's and Pendlebury bridges, and this was the part they particularly wished to examine. However, before 8 am the water was largely cleared and 140 people were there to make the search.

They used iron spades, barrows, rakes, riddles and planking. Mud was wheeled to adjacent fields, there to be examined and left to be absorbed into the earth. So the fields began to take on their black heaps, and everything proceeded in such an orderly and spirited fashion that Mr Supt Ellison was spurred to offer a reward of £5 to anyone who should discover the missing watch.

"This," as a reporter recorded, "doubtless proved a great incentive to exertion. The scene throughout the day was of the liveliest description, and any tendency which there might have been to monotony was relieved by the distribution of sundry allowances of beer, and also by one or two false alarms that the watch had been found. In one case, the mistake was pardonable, and it was a great disappointment to the workman who thought the £5 was within his grasp to draw from the mud, not the coveted watch, but a steel chain attached to a small pot lid.

"In another instance, a small tin box was mistaken for the silver case. From daylight to dark, the labourers worked with only a few minutes' intermission, but their exertions were not crowned with success, though the mud which had been removed into the fields still had to be overhauled. Soon after 5 pm the task was completed and the navvies were dismissed to their homes. There was a strong body of police in attendance during the day from Wigan, Bolton and Warrington districts [together with] Mr Supt Ellison, Mr Inspector Peters, from Wigan, Supt Jackson, from Wigan, and Inspector Reid from Farnworth. The Assistant Chief Constable, Captain Palmer, was also present during the morning. The ones of this party were cared for at the police station at Pendlebury Bridge, a small cottage whereat an officer had been on duty ever since the order for the search was given, and where, shortly after, an immense potato pie appeared upon the scene.

"There was an incessant stream of spectators to and from the canal all through the day. During the forenoon, Pendlebury Bridge was black with the heads of those who had come to witness the search, and towards the afternoon, as the navvies progressed with the work, Gibson Bridge presented a similar appearance. Nearly a couple of hundredweight of eels were caught by means of nets placed at the spots where the canal was tapped as well as a large quantity of small fish, which were placed in Adlington reservoir. Several residents of Pendlebury Row saved a few shillings by this."

Earnest and enjoyable that search might have been; but it was wasted. The watch was not in the canal at all.

Chapter Eight

Enter Thomas Grime

WHILE John Healey and Thomas Walton awaited their trial at Liverpool Assizes, a young Chorley man read of the searching of the canal for a watch and found, to his surprise, and certainly to his horror, that it was in his possession. He consulted his father. The discovery implicated his brother, then serving three years' penal servitude in Dartmoor for the theft of a horse blanket. They decided to go to Wigan and hand the watch to police.

This is where Thomas Grime, the man subsequently hanged for the murder of James Barton, enters the story: for he was the criminal held in Dartmoor.

He was brought to Wigan and lodged in the gaol at Pemberton.

"Rumours are as to a confession alleged to have been made by Grime," declared the Wigan newspaper, "but on this point we can not give any trustworthy information, for nothing has been allowed to transpire on the subject. It is, however, well known that Inspector Peters proceeded to Barrow-in-Furness at the beginning of the present week and that he brought with him, in custody, a person who was in some way implicated by Grime. This man, too, is in Pemberton lock-up."

The latest twist in affairs led to Healey and Walton appearing before Mr Justice Mellor at Liverpool Assizes. Mr Aspinall, QC, applied for a further postponement of a hearing "in view of the facts which have recently been brought to light." The judge felt that, in the circumstances, he ought to postpone the trial until the next Assizes, but this was not to the prisoner Walton's liking. He said he would rather go at once to the scaffold than be detained in gaol. He also declared that there was not a word of truth in the story he had told of his part in the murder; that he was drunk at the time; and that he did not recollect a word he had uttered.

Healey, meanwhile, was ill and had to sit in the dock. When he went below, he did so only with assistance.

On his arrival at Pemberton from Dartmoor, Grime was alleged to have made a series of statements which, with hindsight, were extremely significant. According to these preliminary statements, Grime is supposed to have admitted that he *was* present when Barton was killed, but declared that it was a companion of his, William Thompson, a brickmaker, who was the actual murderer; also, that a third accomplice named Joseph Seddon, the last of three, had recently died. Thompson was the man brought from Barrow in Furness by Inspector Peters.

The two prisoners duly appeared in the dock at Wigan's Moot Hall. As ever, it was recorded that "Mr Mayhew watched the case as the representative of the Earl of Crawford, the owner of the pit where the murder was committed." Mr Mayhew was ever an assiduous listener and never failed to get publicity for his pains.

Many relatives of the murdered man were present in court and when Grime was detailing "in the most self-possessed manner the share he had in the horrible deed," one of the dead man's sons had to leave the hall, emotionally drained.

Grime, 30, appeared handcuffed and in convict dress. He was 5ft 6 ins, with fresh complexion, light brown hair and blue eyes. He looked pale, but not over-concerned by what was going on. He was, it was stated, a blacksmith by trade, married, and with one child.

Thompson was muscular and broad in build, probably a few years younger than Grime, and very nearly the same height. He, too, was cool and at times heard the evidence with near indifference. He was said to have denied the truth of the confession of his fellow prisoner. Again, the witnesses were trooped before the magistrates to re-create the minute detail of Barton's murder: the blood, the fires, the timings. Then came the nub of the matter: Grime's apparent confession, read to the court by Inspector Peters:

"I met William Thompson about a fortnight before the murder of Barton near my parents' house in Eaves Lane, Chorley. He then said to me, 'Wilt thou go with me to murder Mr Barton?' We had some ale together in the day, and during the day he asked me if I would go out poaching with him. We met Joseph Seddon the same night, near The Castle in Chorley. Seddon and me refused to go with Thompson to Bawk House Pit at Haigh that night.

"Seddon, Thompson and me met together again about half past nine [one] night in Chorley. We then came forward . . . up the canal bank to Red Rock Bridge, [over the bridge], through [a farmyard] and up the tram road which goes to Bawk House Pit.

"On getting to the pit, Thompson said he would do the old bugger as Barton had denied him of taking game and had ordered him off the premises and told that if he ever came again he would 'do' him.

"Thompson went into the cabin, and at this time the engine was running and pumping water. I was on the pit brow close to the cabin, and Seddon was a few yards further on. Barton was laid down on the form in the cabin. Thompson took a crowbar with both hands, raised it to his shoulders, and said, 'Now you old bugger, I'll do you,' and at the same time struck [Barton] on his forehead with the bar. I heard Barton groan. Thompson said, 'He is not dead,' then gave him another blow with the bar. After he had struck the second blow [Barton] never moved. Thompson got hold of him by the legs and dragged him out of the cabin and chucked him down the slack hole. I moved about six yards further back. Thompson shouted, 'Is there someone coming?' Then he said to Seddon, 'What shall we do with him?' Seddon did not speak. Thompson then said, 'We will put him in the firehole.' Thompson and Seddon put him in the firehole.

"Thompson said to me, 'He will never be seen no more . . . I'll chuck [throw] about ten shovels of slack on him.' He then closed the doors. I was all of a tremble. We all three, Thompson, Seddon and me, crossed the fields and went on the high road that goes up Tuckers Hill and on Blackrod Road. Then we came up an old lane [and onto] the turnpike road and through Adlington to Chorley. We got there about 5 am in the morning. My father asked me where I had been, but I did not tell him. [Later] my father said, 'Keep out of Thompson's company.' He said Thompson was a blackguard. He had several times been in our house and my father had ordered him out.

"After Thompson killed Barton, he took Barton's watch and chain and put them in his pocket. I had a watch of my own. Thompson said that if I would give him my watch and ten shillings, we could divide [the value of] Barton's watch between Seddon and me. I refused. Thompson kept Barton's watch a week, then gave it to Joseph Seddon to pawn. Seddon pawned the watch in the name of John Wallwork and got a sovereign for it. Thompson got ten shillings of the money, and myself and Seddon got five shillings each. We all then went and had a quart or two of ale apiece. Seddon said to me, 'The murder will be found out before long.' Thompson said, 'It will never be found unless some of us splits.' "

Grime apparently signed this statement and later asked to speak to Inspector Peters. "Where," he asked, "is Stepper [a reference to Walton, the man held in Liverpool for trial]? Because he was with us when the murder was committed. Thompson and me, about three or four days before the murder, were poaching beside the paper mill. Stepper (sometimes called Hopper; some calls him Patten) was with us. Stepper was in the cabin when Thompson knocked [Barton] down. Stepper helped drag him across the pit brow to the fireholes. Stepper and Thompson shoved him in the firehole."

This statement, also, was signed.

The next significant evidence came from Grime's brother, James, who unwittingly held the dead man's watch while the canal was being drained in the search for it.

"I am a factory operative and the prisoner is my brother. At the time Mr Barton was murdered, the prisoner was living with us. We both lived with my father. I do not recollect the day or the month when the murder was committed but I know the watch produced. I saw it in the possession of the prisoner a few weeks after the murder. It had no chain on it when he brought it out [in our own home]. It was in a piece of printed rag. He held it in his hands for me to look at, and I said it was a very nice one: was it his own? He said it was. He then put it in his pocket. In a few days, I asked him where he had got it. He [repeated that] it was his own and had suffered for it, and that he had been 12 months in a Liverpool gaol. He brought it out in that manner several times during a fortnight, and before he began wearing it properly. He lent it to me one Sunday, and I wore it. I gave it back to him on the Monday. He wore it himself, lent it to me again, and finally it did not go right. I took it to Henry Barker, watch dresser, in Chorley, and the prisoner fetched it home himself and wore it.

"I know the number of the watch and the make: 17844, and the maker's name, Robert Croskell, Liverpool. I heard the prisoner say he would have the name taken off the watch and his own put on; and have the numbers out."

The watch went into pawn and pawn tickets were twice lost. When his brother was sentenced to three years for stealing a horse cloth:

"I went to Miles Alston's shop, where the watch was pawned. I gave a description of the watch and got an affidavit from Alston, and got it signed by Mr Rigby, the magistrate. I paid 24s-odd and took [the watch] out of pawn and went home."

He wore the watch for a few months, then passed it on to a friend, John Ackers, in a deal involving clothing and money. Then he read in a newspaper about the murdered man's missing watch and "went quite cold" when he realised that the two were the same. "I came to the number 17844 [and read] the paper to my father." He bought back the watch from his friend and his father and he took it to police at Wigan.

Thomas Grime had one comment on all that: "This is not the watch I suffered for: it was a watch got in Preston."

His father, William, a quarryman, then gave evidence:

"I recollect the night James Barton was murdered. I was at home that night. I went out next morning about 5 am. I met my son, Thomas Grime, coming in just as I was going out. I do not recollect whether I spoke to him or not. I did not notice anything about him. My son was not the best of characters at that time, and when I heard of Mr Barton's murder it made me recollect it, for I was afraid he had been in it. I heard of Barton's murder the day after, or the day but one after, it happened, but can not tell exactly. I never had the watch produced in my hand until James brought it back from John Ackers."

Then, the following interchange:

Prisoner: "Father, your statements have been correct so far as you have gone. Do you recollect me being many a time with William Thompson, and you checked me for it?"

Witness: "I recollect you being with him, but not to be a companion of his."

Prisoner: "Do you recollect him coming to our house drunk, and you ordering him out?"

Witness: "I don't know. I never allowed drunken company in my house."

Prisoner: "You was not sure I was up all night was you?"

Witness: "Thou was not in when I got up."

Prisoner: "My father's evidence is right so far as it has gone, but he had advised me to keep out of Thompson's company, and has often given me good advice."

Grime then gave testimony – substantially the same as in his statement to the police – but with some intriguing extra detail:

"Joseph Seddon and me returned to Chorley. Thompson went Bolton road. He told me he was searched that night, at least in the morning. He said two policemen searched him and found on him the watch and two knives – Barton's knife and his own, a black-shafted one."

The police were apparently satisfied with Thompson's explanation. They let him go. "He told me if they had locked him up we would all three have been taken."

Then: "He [Thompson] was the very first man as ever mentioned about murdering anybody. I was present when he murdered Mr Barton. I was present on the ground and no other person murdered him but Thompson."

Thompson declared the statement by Grime to be false.

Handcuffs were removed from Grime so that he could sign his statement. When he had written his name, he said: "I must have something else in this case. Stepper can given evidence that can clear me. He can clear me that I did not lay a hand on Mr Barton."

He was committed to Liverpool Assizes.

What, then, of Thompson?

He was represented by a Mr Hilton who, when told that the prisoner was charged with suspicion of being concerned in murder, said: "We deny it. When he was apprehended, he made a statement which no doubt you will have."

Inspector Peters then said that, when charged with murder, Thompson said he was as innocent "as that piece of timber" and "also as that candle" (pointing to a candle on the table at the time).

Thompson was remanded and he and Grime went to Kirkdale Gaol by train, travelling to the Lancashire and Yorkshire station from the court by cab, which proceeded rapidly through the town centre escorted by half a dozen policemen and followed by a crowd, which shouted and hooted all the way.

Chapter Nine

Appealing to logic

ON MONDAY, August 13, 1866, at 10 am,Thomas Grime faced his judge, Baron Martin, at Liverpool Assizes charged with being concerned in the murder of James Barton. The court was "densely crowded as soon as it became known that the celebrated case was, at last, under investigation."

Grime appeared cool and confident. He declared himself to be "Not guilty," in a firm and decisive voice. There was a second charge: that of stealing the watch of the dead man, or with receiving it knowing it to have been stolen. To this charge, he also pleaded not guilty.

In the dock, too, was Walton. Nine months of prison life had drained any colour from his face and his cheeks were thinner. He had a brief chance to stare around court before being ordered below during Grime's trial.

The jury was sworn: twelve men, one only (Aaron Stock) from the Haigh neighbourhood.

Mr Aspinall, QC, for the prosecution, detailed the – by now – familiar story of how James Barton came to die at the Bawk House Pit except that, in outlining the prosecution case, he made an aside while reading Grime's statement to the police (dealing with the circumstances of the murder) in these terms:

"I must say that you will hear a great deal about William Thompson. So far as these inquiries have resulted, we have been able to obtain no evidence whatsoever of the truth of this story as far as it related to William Thompson. We know nothing inconsistent with the story. We have obtained nothing which goes to incriminate William Thompson. We know nothing whether we favour it or not."

Both statements made by Grime in the lock-up (and already described in detail here) were read and Mr Aspinall told the jury:

"You must observe from them that, although the prisoner clearly admits that he was present when the murder was committed, he seems to reserve it most carefully that he did not strike any blow, or take any personal part in it. What I shall have to submit to you is this:

"That if it be proved to you by the statements and by the facts, especially the facts as to the watch; if it be proved to you that the prisoner went with Thompson or anyone else with the common object of committing the murder which was afterwards committed, it is immaterial who struck the blow.

"If several parties went for the purpose of committing a murder, and all the time aided by their presence if in no other way, I shall have to submit to you that the prisoner must be said to have been guilty of murder."

The first witness, Hannah Pilkington, daughter of James Barton, identified the missing watch which "he had in his pocket whenever he went to work." She added, "I have had it in my hands when making his bed."

Some time later – after other witnesses – William Grime, father of the accused man, recalled how his son arrived home the morning after the murder "just as I was setting off for work. I had three-quarters of a mile to go and had to be there by daylight."

James Bradshaw, a watchmaker in Wigan, made bankrupt in 1862, said he repaired Barton's watch. "It was in the habit of stopping on its back, and I scraped the cap and I believe I put this screw in. The marks of the scraping of the cap are there now."

Police Inspector Peters spoke of bringing Grime back to Lancashire: "When we were about fifty or sixty miles from Dartmoor, he said, 'I saw you on the pit brow the Sunday morning after the murder was committed.' I was there on the Sunday morning.

The inspector recalled taking a statement from Grime at Pemberton police station. "I took it down from his mouth, and he said it in the presence of others of whom the superintendent was one. On my oath, I did not ask him to make the statement. He said he wanted to see me and the warder came for me. I did not go to him in the cell. He was brought to me in the office where the superintendent was. I had been to Barrow to apprehend Thompson, who is mentioned in that statement, and on my return it appeared [that Grime] heard my voice and called to tell me he wanted to speak to me.

"I said, 'What do you want, Grime?' and he replied, 'Where's Stepper now, because he was with us when we committed the murder.' He then made a further statement which I took down in writing. I read that over. He signed it. This is it."

Mr Pope (counsel for the prisoner): "You just now used an

expression which was not correct. You should be a little more careful. The expression used was, 'Where's Stepper, for he was the man with us when we committed the murder?' Those were not the words. The words were, 'He was with us when the murder was committed'."

The inspector referred to the statement – "Yes, those are the words. There is no difference."

Mr Pope retorted: "There is a great deal of difference. From first to last did he not always endeavour to fix the murder upon Thompson, and express himself simply to have been present, taking no part?"

"He did."

The second statement was then read and put in by the Clerk and the witness was re-examined by Mr Pope.

"You have been concerned in this case from the beginning?"

"I have."

"Making inquiries for the past two or three years?"

"Yes."

"A reward was offered – £100 by the crown and £200 by Lord Balcarras, owner of the pit, for the discovery of the offenders and a Queen's pardon to any accomplice not the actual criminal?"

"Yes."

"There have been three confessions?" (There were, of course, four, but the first was properly considered to be of no account.)

"Yes. One by a man named Healey, now dead; another by a man named Walton, and now this one by Grime."

"And, with reference to all of them, you, in the exercise of your duty, have sought about for evidence to corroborate the various stories?"

"I have."

"With reference to the statements this man made at various times, have you endeavoured to ascertain beyond possession of the watch whether there are any other statements you can corroborate?"

"I have."

"For instance, he [Grime] made some statement about Thompson having been searched on the way to Bolton by two police officers. Have you found anything of that?"

"No."

"You have made inquiries from Bolton police?"

"I have."

"You can get no information as to whether or not it happened?"

"I cannot. I gave information at the time to Bolton police about the loss of a knife and watch and other things, I suppose. Yes."

"Therefore, their attention would be directed at that very time to the loss of a watch and a knife?"

"Yes."

Mr Aspinall: "Who is called Stepper?"

The inspector: "Thomas Walton."

"This man who is now confined?"

"Yes."

"My friend wishes me to ask you, was it in consequence of Stepper's confession that the canal was searched?"

"It was."

The case for the prosecution was closed.

Mr Pope then rose to reply on behalf of the prisoner. He said, "I do not think it has ever been my misfortune to be engaged in a case which presses more heavily upon me than this case. When one looks at the horrible character of the crime – a crime one would hope is almost unparalleled in the history of this country; [and when] one considers what the results of this inquiry may be for the man who stands upon his trial [when] it is to the statement by himself that the prosecution looked for the purpose of fixing guilt upon him, one can not help feel that there are difficulties, and very grave difficulties, in the case both for you and for myself."

The jury's sympathies would be with Barton. Their antipathy would be towards Grime. Knowing this, he had, nevertheless, to ask them to look calmly and coldly at the evidence: in other words, he was appealing to logic, not emotion.

"Now, gentlemen, it is very difficult indeed to account for all the workings of the human mind. One can not exactly understand what particular motive it can be which seems to prompt men of criminal disposition to confess, or to declare themselves guilty, of enormous or horrible crimes with which, in fact, they have nothing to do.

"Without referring to all the circumstances which have occurred again and again in the history of our criminal jurisprudence, [you will recall that] men of diseased imagination, or morbid and corrupt vanity, for the sake of notoriety, or from some motive which, to sound and sane and healthy men, is almost inexplicable, have confessed themselves guilty even of crimes which have never been committed.

"In this case, the very first difficulty in determining whether this man is to be hanged on his own confession is that he is the third man who has confessed to this crime. And with the exception of the possession of this watch, there is no more corroboration of that story he states himself than there is of the stories told by two other men, about whom nobody now says a word.

"One of these men is now dead, and nobody, of course [sic], wishes to say a word about him. With regard to the second, you have it on the evidence as shown by counsel for the prosecution that the man Stepper, alluded to in the process of this case, made some statements which were manifestly untrue. Walton's statement, as a confession, is as worthy of credence – if the thing is worthy of credence – as a confession of Grime."

According to Walton's confession, it was necessary to search the canal for the watch of the murdered man. Plainly this part of his story was false. But it was, nevertheless, true that murder had taken place. How were they to account for that? If they were not to rely on Walton's confession, could they rely on Grime's? – "a confession made three years after the event by a man whose mind is not in that healthy condition which a mind untainted by vice would be; a man to whom it would seem to be a sort of criminal glory to be associated with crimes like this; a man who – not like you, who would recoil from having anything like this crime added to your reputation; a man attached to the criminal classes, whose ambition it would naturally be to go down to posterity as a great and glorious man?"

A curious argument, the reader might think, but one, no doubt, that a Victorian jury would expect. Grime was presumably "tainted by vice" because of minor theft, and attached to "the criminal classes" because of his association with drifters in search of a hare for the family pot. As for his "ambition to go down to posterity as a great and glorious man," there is not the slightest suggestion in Grime's actions or statements that this is so. Mr Pope's flight of fancy was to have little effect in discrediting all that Grime had previously said.

"I ask you [counsel continued] if you can rely on the statements this man makes; and I ask you how you are to credit these statements any more than the statements of the others. Nay, more: When you come to see the nature of the statements he makes, you will see that these observations, general rather than particular, are worthy of your consideration. You will remember that this man was at large after the murder was committed. He was perfectly well aware of all that had been stated, and done, and written in newspapers, and advertised about the matter. He knew very well when the police officer came to charge him [of] this reward of £100 by the government and £200 by Lord Balcarres to anybody who would fix the murder on anybody else; and of a Queen's pardon for anybody who, having not committed the crime, would confess to participation in the crime."

There was, therefore, not only the motive of notoriety, but the motive supplied by the knowledge that, by making this statement, he could keep himself clear of the gallows, and might obtain the money.

"You find he makes precisely the statement you would expect; you find all this to account for it; and you find no other evidence in the case but his own statement tending to fix it with the murder. I ask you to look upon that statement with the gravest possible doubt, and to deal with it in the way in which you would deal with it supposing it to have been made in the witness box with regard to anybody else, instead of being made to the policeman with regard to himself."

Counsel was not asking the jury to consider Grime's confession in a light which was improper, or inconsistent, with the view the law took of statements of that kind. "You will ask yourselves, very carefully, if this statement be believed by the prosecution."

Why was Thompson not in the dock with Grime?

"The reason is simple. The law provides that no man shall be convicted only on the uncorroborated statement of a man who is, or appears to be, an accomplice; and the reason he is not there is that no corroboration is found which leads materially to incriminate Thompson.

"Far be it for me to throw out any hint that Thompson is the guilty man. It is not part of my duty. But when considering the question whether you are to convict a man on his own confession, look at it in this light: If Thompson were in the dock, and Grime in the box to tell you his story, the law would say that you must not rely on the story Grime told you unless it was corroborated in important particulars. And why is this? Because of the motives likely to actuate the mind of man to induce him to make false statements. And if this be true with regard to Thompson, it is equally true with regard to Grime."

In cross-examination, very little of the evidence was questioned.

"That Barton was murdered outright is true. That his watch was some weeks afterwards in the possession of the prisoner may be equally true. And that the prisoner made certain statements to the police officer is likewise true. But whether that is enough to convict him of the murder is another and a different matter."

The watch was not recognised until March, 1866, more than three years after the event. That fact alone would weaken a case very much if it were only one of larceny.

"This possession is the only direct evidence against Grime [and it] is some weeks after the murder. This, I venture to submit, is not a very strong point against him. Charged with stealing the watch, or receiving it knowing it to have been stolen – this would be a strong point, but still it does not make him a murderer. It may make him a receiver of property which has been dishonestly taken, but it does not, in any way, connect him with the act of violence, or in any way bring him on the spot."

If the jury could not rely on Grime's confession, he doubted whether it would find a verdict "by which the life of a fellow creature will be sacrificed."

Then he added, "Supposing you accept his statement to be true: What does it amount to? If you are satisfied that this man, Grime, went to the coal pit with the intention of murdering Barton; or if you are of the opinion that he aided and abetted the murderers, or watched while they committed the crime so as to render active assistance, he is as much guilty of the murder as if he had struck the blow.

"If you come to the conclusion that he was not there with the common intent; or that being there, he was accidentally present and saw what was done, he is neither guilty of the murder, nor can he be convicted, although guilty of the shameful conduct of witnessing the crime and giving no information. I will take other words than my own – 'If a man happens to be present at murder and takes no part in it, nor endeavoureth to prevent it, nor apprehend the murderer, nor levy hue and cry after him, the strange behaviour of his, although highly criminal, would not, of itself, render him to be a principal or accessory.' What I ask you to consider with regard to this matter is this: Take it, consider it, read it, weigh it, see it to be true if you will – Does it amount to more than this; that happening to be present at the time when Thompson murdered James Barton, he took no part in it, nor endeavoured to prevent it, nor apprehended the murderer, nor levied hue or cry after him, but accepted, if you please, at the end some hush money to hold his tongue? If that be the fact, then he is not guilty of the murder."

It would be manifestly unfair if the jury should imply anything in the confession which was not expressed. Prosecution counsel had said that as far as he could make out, the man had scrupulously avoided stating that he was party to the murder. The most he had said was that he was present at the time the murder was committed. He [counsel] did not suppose that Inspector Peters intended, for one moment, to do any injustice to Grime when he used the words, "Stepper was present when we committed the murder," as if Grime had associated himself with the murder as a joint act. But when the jury looked at all the words from his mouth, they would find that Grime never said, and never intended to say, "when we committed the murder." He said he was there "when the murder was committed."

"Gentlemen, there is a great distinction.

"This is not a case in which I can ask you for any sympathy with the prisoner; a man who was scoundrel and wretch enough to stand by and see a horrible crime committed. You may loathe him, but you are not to send him to the gallows because he was standing on the pit brow on the night of the murder; nor yet because he was wretch enough, having seen the murder, to accept the price of blood; to screen the murder which had been committed. He is charged with consenting to, and aiding, the murder of Barton. If he was merely present, and, like a sneaking coward, took no part in the murder, then he is not guilty."

He challenged the jury to look through the whole of Grime's statement and find anything in it that would bear any other complexion. It would not be fair to take part of it and not the whole. There was not one word in which Grime admitted himself to have had any hand in the murder. The murder was proposed to him, but he declared that he refused to have anything to do with it. His purpose in going out on the night Barton died was not to murder, but to poach, an act in which he was likely to be associated with Thompson. In the course of their poaching, they might easily find themselves on the pit bank; and when there, according to the statement, Thompson – and only he – did the deed.

"You have no evidence that Thompson did it but this statement. You have no evidence that the prisoner was there but this statement. If you take that statement to prove he was on the spot, you must also take it to prove what he did on the spot. His story [declares] that he did see Thompson do it, but that he [Grime] had no interference or hand in it. There is not one syllable tending to fasten any guilt upon him except [that] of having been present at the commission of the crime without having the courage to prevent it. If that be the theory you take, then I must ask you to acquit the prisoner.

"If I accept his statement, as I put it to you, it also accounts entirely for the possession of the watch without his having been guilty of the murder. He represents himself as having come into possession of the watch afterwards – as hush money to say nothing about the murder – because the thing would never have been found out honestly. Gentlemen, I have nothing whatever to say to you as an appeal to your feelings. I can only appeal to your sense of justice. I said this was a case of great difficulty to myself. It is so. The only defence I can offer, if you accept that confession at all, is that you should conceive this man to be an even more craven scoundrel than the man who, you might also say, had the good courage to do the act.

"It may be, perhaps, that the real truth with regard to this mysterious matter may never be disclosed before a human tribunal. We have already heard that one, at least, of the unhappy men who confessed to having been guilty of this murder has passed to another, and higher tribunal, where the judgment, at least, will be unerring. For us, gentlemen, we can merely apply to the facts of the case such powers as our limited judgments may give us."

In other words, what defence counsel were urging was that, if the jury came to the conclusion that Grime was actively, and of his own intention, aiding and abetting in murder, they must convict without hesitation. But if they doubted it; if they took his statement as truth – that he was present, but not aiding or abetting, not interfering, not dealing with it as a man of courage or character would do, but simply standing by, looking on – then they must acquit him; "and remember, if you do come to that conclusion, that your verdict will not be one which weakly allows a great criminal to escape; but, by holding fast to the great principle that no man shall be convicted except upon conclusive evidence, you will be strengthening the foundation of that justice, the administration of which is at once our national glory and the admiration of the civilised world."

The judge then began his summing up, but was imperfectly heard in the courtroom, so that what we have of his words is an interpretation rather than a near-verbatim account.

In order that Grime might be found guilty (he said), the jury must be satisfied that he was more than an innocent spectator when the murder was committed. If they should think that he went out knowing that the man was to be murdered, that he was not the actual murderer, and that, after the deed was committed, he took possession of part of the property acquired in the course of the murder and converted it, and sold it, then let them ask themselves, as sensible men, whether he was not there along with Thompson, and was just as guilty as Thompson.

If two or three or more went together for the purpose of committing a crime, the man who was there and did nothing was just as guilty as the man who struck the blow. Why was Thompson not standing at the bar? The answer was really obvious: there was not a particle of evidence against Thompson except the statement of the prisoner, and that, no evidence against him whatever. There was another man in custody on the charge of this crime and the reason he had not been before them to be tried was this: that Grime had made a statement it was considered unfair for them to know with regard to the other prisoner if they had been trying him. They must dismiss the question with regard to Thompson from their minds. This was also the reason why no evidence had yet been tendered against the other prisoner, and why it was thought advisable to try the prisoners separately.

It might be (as had been argued) that there had been some remarkable confessions in the past. It might be that persons had made confessions of great guilt when they were innocent, but he thought this must be a very extraordinary thing. It must be quite out of the ordinary that a man, after the expiration of three years, would say he was guilty of a thing he was not guilty of at all. The judge thought that must be the exception and not the rule.

He continued by saying that it must be a most extraordinary thing if such a statement as this were untrue when a man came forward not once, or twice, but three times and said he had been concerned in the murder. Because persons had made confessions in the past who were not guilty, they must not consequently look upon this statement as false, also. The jury would consider Grime's statement as they would consider any other. They must put the most reasonable construction upon it; ascertain its true meaning; and if they believed it false they would dismiss it. But they must ask whether it was reasonable, or probable, that a man should make a statement of that kind if it were not true.

The judge then dealt at length with evidence about events at the time of the murder and subsequently, as told by the various witnesses:

If (he said) evidence of the watch were true, there was no doubt that the prisoner was in possession shortly after the murder. The judge was therefore far from saying that there was no evidence against Grime other than that in the man's own evidence. There was no more common evidence of a crime than that a person was in possession of stolen property shortly after it had been stolen; and he was not aware that it was no evidence of complicity in murder when the stolen watch was found in the prisoner's possession a few weeks after the crime. He did not think, therefore, that counsel was justified in telling the jury that there was no evidence against Grime other than his own confession. However, this was not necessarily sufficient to convict Grime of the murder. It was an exception for a man to state he was guilty of a crime which he had not committed, but he must leave that question in the jury's hands.

It was here that the judge made his quaint reference to Dartmoor prison, where Grime had been held, as "one of those large places where criminals are confined in the South of England."

The jury must ask themselves, the judge continued, what they thought of the story that Grime was standing by and seeing a foul and dastardly crime committed without raising his hand to the assistance of the murdered man. The story of Thompson being searched by police after the murder might be true, or not true. It might be that a policeman had the watch in his hand; but they had nothing more to show than the statement by the prisoner that Thompson had told him he was searched.

The jury must judge whether the prisoner was a mere bystander or whether he did not go into "this place with this Thompson" to murder; and whether the two went with a common purpose, even though the murder was not by Grime's hand. If Grime went with the common intent of committing murder, then it seemed to the judge both reasonable, and common sense, that he was, in the eyes of the law, as guilty as the man who struck the blows. If the jury disbelieved the whole of Grime's story, and thought he was not there at all, then there was an end to the case.

The jury took no more than two minutes to reach its verdict: GUILTY.

Thomas Grime was asked: "What have you to say why sentence of death should not be passed upon you?"

He replied in a low, firm voice: "I am as innocent as a child."

The judge donned a black cap and said:

"Thomas Grime, you have been found guilty of this murder upon, to my mind, as satisfactory evidence as if I had seen you with my own eyes commit it, and I have not the slightest doubt that you accompanied somebody – for I will say nothing with regard to Thompson – but somebody; and it is likely and probable, that if your own hand did not strike the blow, you were just as guilty as the man who did it. You went there for the purpose of [James Barton] being murdered and you took part in the proceeds of this watch, which was taken from him.

"A more barbarous murder was never proved in a court of law, and if the punishment of death is to be continued at all, a case more worthy of it has never been proved than that which has been proved here today. The circumstances of the case have been stated, and put so particularly, that there is no occasion for me to repeat them. I do not want to harrow you by a detail of them, or pain myself, but I shall at once proceed to pass upon you the sentence which the law directs. I do beseech you to take advantage of the opportunity given to you to make your peace with God, for I can hold out no hope to you of any remission of the sentence.

"The sentence of the law is that, for the crime of wilful murder, you will be taken from hence to the prison from whence you came, and taken from thence to a place of execution, and be there hanged by the neck until you are dead, and that your body then be taken down and buried within the precincts of the gaol from whence you were taken. May the Lord have mercy on your soul."

Grime, who had remained composed – "perfectly stolid" – throughout the proceedings, was then removed from the dock.

Chapter Ten

A case "worthy of death"

A T THIS DISTANCE in time, it would seem that, once Grime had made his confession, his eventual fate was assured. He would make his statement without having the caution given to people today. He was unable to give evidence at Assizes because he was not, in the manner of the times, judged to be a competent witness for the defence. His presence with a killer implied that he was also acting with malice.

Let us look, here, at some of the ways in which style and the law differed.

First, the curious title of the judge: Baron Martin. Before the Judicature Acts, judges of the Court of Exchequer were called barons, and the chief judge of that court was styled the Lord Chief Baron of the Exchequer. It was originally a court having jurisdiction only in matters concerning public revenue but this responsibility widened.

Next, the statements. In 1906, the chief constable of Birmingham was concerned that on the same circuit, one judge had censured an officer of his for having cautioned a prisoner, while another had censured a constable for not having done so.

As a result of his writing to the then Lord Chief Justice, Lord Alverstone, a set of judges' rules came into being. When a police officer had reasonable grounds for supposing that someone had committed an offence, he must caution that person in these words: "You are not obliged to say anything unless you wish to do so, but what you say may be put into writing and given in evidence."

Where someone was charged with, or informed that he might be prosecuted for, an offence, he must be told: "Do you wish to say anything? You are not obliged to say anything unless you wish to do so, but whatever you say will be taken down in writing and may be used in evidence."

Grime, of course, had neither of these benefits. Had he elected not to make a statement implicating himself, it would appear that there was evidence only of his having had possession of James Barton's watch.

Before the Criminal Evidence Act of 1898, a defendant could not even give evidence on his own behalf. The new Act meant that, with certain qualifying conditions, "every person charged with an offence, and the wife or husband, as the case may be, of the person so charged, shall be a competent witness for the defence at every stage of the proceedings, whether the person so charged is charged solely or jointly with any other person."

Where a defendant gives evidence in the witness box, the Crown is entitled to gain from him evidence which may incriminate his co-defendants.

It was not until the Homicide Act of 1957 that the doctrine of constructive or implied malice was in operation: that is, "killing in the course of a violent or dangerous felony . . . was murder even in the absence of any intent to kill or cause grievous bodily harm."

In Grime's case, it could have been forcibly argued (as it was in a case after the 1957 Act), that "two men may embark on an unlawful joint enterprise, but one may go far beyond the scope of that joint enterprise and commit something beyond the contemplation or foresight of the second man. In that event, the second man would not, in law, be responsible for the act of the first, which went right outside the bounds or scope of their unlawful joint enterprise, and beyond what could be contemplated or foreseen by the second man."

This would reflect the situation when Thompson and Grime set out to poach on the night of James Barton's death in 1863.

If, on the other hand, Grime "must have contemplated or foreseen" that Thompson might kill during their "joint enterprise," he would be open to conviction of murder.

Back in Grime's home town, the leader writer of the *Chorley Standard* took up his pen:

"The judge, in passing sentence, warned the prisoner that he could hold out to him no hope of any remission of his sentence, but at the same time, a careful reader can not fail to find in his remarks ground for hope. According to one account, Baron Martin is represented as saying, 'A more barbarous murder never was committed, and if the punishment of death is to be continued there is no case more worthy of it than this.'

"Another account has the sentence thus, 'A more barbarous murder was never proved in a court of law, and if the punishment of death is to be inflicted at all, a case more worthy of it never was proved.'

"Now who can fail to perceive that a hint is not here thrown out that capital punishment may shortly be abolished? Several men of good weight have lately declared themselves to be in favour of the abolition of capital punishment, and we may, perhaps, be nearer such an alteration in the law than many suppose. Notwithstanding, we can not fail to admit with Baron Martin that if ever a crime deserved the extreme punishment allowed by the law, this is most certainly one, for a more cold-blooded and inhuman tragedy can scarcely be conceived. Recent events, however, have clearly shown that there is a disposition at headquarters to commute the capital sentence. Only last week, intelligence was received that the sentence against Banks [a Preston murderer] had been [sic] reprieved, and yet in his case, Baron Martin, alluding to the cruelty manifested, spoke quite as strongly.

"Moreover, we should remember that in Grime's case, not one tittle of evidence has been advanced to show the part he took in the murder. In the absence of such evidence, we may charitably suppose that Grime did not take any active part, and although this does not lessen his guilt, we may, with some show of reason, expect that any communication to the Home Secretary on his behalf might meet with a favourable response. So far as we can yet see, however, it appears certain that Grime will undergo the last dread sentence of the law, and it now behoves him to make good use of the advice tendered to him by Baron Martin to make ready for that place from which no traveller returns."

Grime's mother was interviewed at her home in Eaves Lane, Chorley. She was "broken-hearted", had scarcely eaten for three weeks, and "she does not appear to have the least wish to visit [Grime], knowing the effect it would have upon her." Her husband, meanwhile, "looked thin and ill." Strangely, there is again no mention here of Grime's wife.

Shortly after Grime's case had been heard, Mr Aspinall, prosecuting QC, and the judge conferred about Walton's case. Subsequently, Mr Aspinall said that "Thomas Walton is not defended by any counsel, my Lord, and if we are entirely in your Lordship's hands as to the course to be taken with him, we will do whatever you think best."

The judge asked Walton whether he wished to be tried at the next Assizes. Walton preferred to be tried more immediately, at the present Assizes.

Later that day, Mr Aspinall said that, as his Lordship was aware, the prisoner was charged with the same murder as that of which Grime had already been convicted. Having had the case a long time in counsel's hands, he had, of course, given it every consideration, and he might say that it rested entirely upon the confession of the prisoner himself.

The prisoner, however, made a confession under very different circumstances to those under which Grime confessed; for he was not sober at the time, and he contradicted what he had said almost immediately afterwards.

The case had been postponed to find out whether what the prisoner had stated could be corroborated; but far from corroboration, there was contradiction. Under the circumstances, he could not hope to obtain a satisfactory result if the prisoner were tried, and therefore, he did not propose to offer any evidence for the prosecution.

The judge thought counsel had taken a sound view and he felt that a satisfactory conviction could not be obtained. As far as he was concerned, Mr Aspinall might safely take the matter in his own hands.

Mr Aspinall: "Perhaps your Lordship will allow a verdict of acquittal to be taken."

Answer: "Yes."

No evidence was, therefore, offered against Walton, who had been in custody for nine months. The judge told him: "You know best whether you are guilty of this murder, but whether or not, the prosecution thought proper to offer no evidence against you. You are, therefore, discharged."

Chapter Eleven

Preparing earnestly for eternity

THOMPSON, having walked free, finally disappears from public view. He did not have an easy reception from a population still, and for long, long afterwards, incensed by the brutal murder of James Barton. Grime was, in the end, at pains to exonerate others he had named while maintaining his own innocence of physical attack on the dead man.

At this time and distance it is difficult to imagine why he should try the impossible of equating the two, for one thing is certain: Barton is hardly likely to have injured himself and then climbed into his own fire. Looking at the evidence, one can only conclude that Grime's motives were religious in origin. He had nothing to lose and, perhaps, something to gain in eternity if he forgave those who trespassed against him. He was Roman Catholic; and in the pain of his predicament, he turned back to the Church.

For the sequence of events leading from dock to scaffold, we rely on accounts of the time, and particularly on the reporting of the *Wigan Observer,* which had repeatedly filled its columns with long accounts of the affair and everything surrounding it.

"We are informed [it stated] that Grime seems to be earnestly preparing himself for eternity. He spends a greater portion of the brief space of time remaining to him in the perusal of religious books and in devotional exercise. Whilst he pays the utmost attention to the exhortations of his spiritual adviser, The Reverend Henry Gibson, the chaplain appointed to him (the prisoner confessing the Roman Catholic faith), he carefully avoids all conversation upon the subject of the crime for which he is to suffer. When any officials of the gaol have referred to it in his presence, he has manifested some displeasure, remarking that he did not wish to talk about the past, and desired to fix his thoughts upon that which was to come.

"He speaks calmly, respecting his approaching end, expressing his conviction that when the time comes, he will be prepared to meet his fate manfully and firmly. He was not visited by any of his relatives or friends last week. This may no doubt be accounted for by the unhappy criminal having sent them word that he hoped they would not see him more than once or twice prior to his execution, as the interviews would turn his thoughts from the concerns of his soul.

"He was, of course, removed to Kirkdale Gaol – 'the place from whence he came' – and the Rev Gibson, a zealous and earnest priest, has been unremitting in his attentions to the miserable man. There is no doubt that the latter was brought to a proper sense of the awful position in which he stood. It would certainly be far more satisfactory to the public to know he had made full confession of the crime for which his life had just been forfeited, but he has made none; at least none which will be made public. He evinced so much penitence that Mr Gibson thought himself justified in giving him Holy Communion a few days after his conviction, and the administration of that cheering right has been repeated subsequently.

"He was also visited by the Reverend Canon Greenhalgh of Chorley. That gentleman was the murderer's earliest spiritual counsellor and initiated him into the tenets of the faith of the Roman Church when he was some ten years of age.

"The canon reminded him of his misspent life and exhorted him to repent and to make the most of the short space of time remaining to him. Grime expressed his sorrow for his past conduct and his determination to seek consolation where it was, alone, to be found. It was then, it appears, that he resolved upon exculpating Thompson and Seddon from the charges that he made against them, having heard that in consequence of his statement, ill-feeling had been excited against them among the people at Chorley.

"He informed Captain Gibbs, the governor of the gaol, that he wished to make statements to this effect. The governor declined to receive any confession unless it was made in writing, and upon being supplied with a slate [Grime] wrote a few lines exonerating Thompson, Seddon and Walton from all complicity in the crime. This act seems to have relieved his mind considerably. He became quite composed after it and appeared to pay even still more attention to his spiritual concern. He sent word to his relatives that he trusted they would not go to see him more than once or twice prior to his execution, saying that the interviews would necessarily be of a painful character, and would have the effect of turning his thoughts from the all-important topic, the welfare of his soul.

"In consequence of this message, he received very few visits. We had an interview with his father – a decent-looking old man – but nothing remarkable took place. The criminal had spent a greater portion of his time since his condemnation in the perusal of religious books and devotional exercises.

"On Thursday, the Rev. Gibson was with him at an early hour and the entire day was occupied in acts of devotion. Grime said 'Don't' on his father requesting to see him on the following day; and he also expressed a wish to retain some small pictures of a religious class – some of the saints and martyrs published specially for the use of members of the Roman Catholic Church, that he might present them as remembrances to any of his relatives or friends who might be there during the day. This wish was complied with.

"He repeated the remark that he had made his peace with God and that the only thing which troubled him was the disgrace he had brought upon his family. On Friday his two married sisters, Catherine and Margaret Ratcliffe, along with his brothers, Evan and Richard Grime, and his sister in law, Ellen, proceeded to Liverpool by railway from Coppull. They arrived at Kirkdale about half past ten in the morning and remained with him for about an hour. The meeting was most affecting and sad. His appearance had greatly altered and he was scarcely recognisable by some of his friends.

"He made inquiries after his father, whom he had been particularly expecting. The conversation was almost wholly upon spiritual matters and he manifested entire readiness for death. He assured them that he felt quite happy; that he was confident of forgiveness; and that although he might suffer for a short time, meaning, no doubt, the purgatorial suffering, he would be in heaven before very long. He pointed to the religious emblem suspended from his neck and declared that no one wearing that could fail to obtain salvation.

"His relatives told him Masses would be said for his soul at the chapels in Chorley and in the neighbourhood and this appeared to give him much pleasure. During the interview, he wept frequently, but at the parting he appeared cheerful and warmly shook them by the hand and said he would bid them adieu for the last time in this world. He sent a private message to his father. One of the jailers was present in the cell during the whole of the time, so the conversation was somewhat restrained. The relatives returned from Liverpool the same evening and Grime spent the remaining day in devotion."

The man to whom Grime appears to have confided most in gaol was the scripture reader Francis Satterthwaite.

They had an empathy not apparent in Grime's other relationships. To Satterthwaite, he declared several times that "he never had hands on old Barton;" that "others were more guilty than he was;" though he never formally denied that he was present when murder was done.

On the Saturday of his execution, after he had breakfasted, and the chaplain had been with him, Grime requested a few parting words with his old friend and Satterthwaite was allowed to visit him.

Grime made several statements to the governor, Mr Gibbs, but they are lost to public knowledge, although the words Grime wrote on a slate are known:

"I wish it to be known publicly that what I said at different times about William Thompson, Joseph Seddon and Walton being present at the murder of Barton is not true. They were not present. They had nothing at all to do with it."

Grime went to bed on the eve of his execution at 9.15 pm and rose at about 5.15 am. The chaplain was in his cell at 7.30 am to give Holy Communion. The two spent some time in prayer. The chaplain then read to Grime the recommendations of a departing soul and gave him "the last blessing." Grime ate a hearty breakfast and spent most of the remainder of his time in this life with Satterthwaite. A few minutes before twelve Grime was asked to surrender himself to the executioner. He went from the condemned cell, beneath the chapel, to a room where Calcraft was waiting. There, he was pinioned. Grime submitted patiently and firmly. To the deputy governor, who was among those attending, he said, "Mr Formby, I want to bid you goodbye. Goodbye my friend, and God bless you."

He then shook hands with Formby, having already thanked the governor of the gaol for his kindness and the chaplain for his ministrations. He told the chaplain that he wished to send his love to his father.

A procession was formed and it moved towards the scaffold, Grime walking firmly and without support.

Building of the scaffold at the north-west angle of the gaol's outer wall had begun on the Friday afternoon and Calcraft arrived in the evening. It was completed at an early hour on Saturday, and those who watched came to the conclusion that the drop was so far concealed in "sombre drapery" that little would be seen when Grime met his punishment.

Most of those who arrived for the execution earliest – around 8 am – were from the country; people who had known Grime. Two of the murdered Barton's nephews were among the twenty-five or so who assumed the execution was at 8 am, since that was the normal time for such affairs in Manchester and other places throughout the land. Most of them drifted away to public houses. Some of the earlier arrivals were pit men.

Later arrivals were families in their best clothes, as if on holiday. Trains from Wigan and its neighbourhood were packed. Many hundreds arrived on foot and gathered beneath the gallows as noon approached. There were heavy showers between 9 am and 11 am, so that it was in the last hour that the crowds could be counted by the thousand. Then a warm sun began to dry the long brick wall of the prison and the gallows were etched in sharper relief. The people of Liverpool seemed to enjoy the sun as much as the prospect of an execution, or more; and it was noted that women were not numerous, and some of those who did attend "were not very reputable." The mob was orderly, and the hundred police present had an easy task. The black drapery of the gallows was moving slightly in a breeze. The crowd was growing up to the very last moment, those who were latest running so as not to miss the killing of Tom Grime.

So, at 11.55, Tallow Jack appeared; and at 12.02 Grime and his entourage. Then came a solitary voice in the crowd, "That's the bugger. That's the devil."

Thomas Grime said those last words on earth – "Lord Jesus receive my soul." And so he died, to be buried that afternoon in the precincts of the gaol. Justice was served.

Or so it is said.

Did Thompson believe it?

Did Stepper?

Epilogue

ON a windy February day in 1988, after a night of storms which had left a trail of damaged or felled trees, I made my first visit to Haigh. The weather seemed appropriate to the occasion. There is not much to see at Haigh. It is a sparce community in open, flattish countryside dominated by Haigh Hall, whose owner, at the time of James Barton's murder, would have had a splendid view of the landscape below him, of his pit chimneys, and of the shining ribbon of water formed by the canal. The hall is vast, almost overpoweringly so, and now it is given over, with its grounds, to the public. It was built for a rich family and its true purpose departed with that family.

There are faded little signs everywhere: miniature railway, woodlands, model trains, golf shop, snack bar, picnic area, crazy golf, model village, children's playground, arboretum. Wigan Corporation is the hall's master now and the earl is long gone. Those who, a century ago, would have been given short shrift for being seen there now stroll the pathways and regard them, quite properly, as their own.

The Crawford title is that of the premier earldom of Scotland, created in 1398. In 1848, it was the researches of Alexander William Crawford Lindsay, 25th/8th Earl of Crawford and Balcarres, who was born at Muncaster Castle, Cumberland, that established his father's claim to this title.

The son succeeded to it in 1869 and died at Florence in 1880. He was buried at Dunecht, near Aberdeen. His body was stolen from a mausoleum there and found after some months in a wood.

The present hall was built between 1830 and 1849 by the 24th Earl of Crawford, who drew his own plans. Care was taken not to mine beneath it and the foundry at Haigh provided all the ironwork. Heating required seven boilers for hot air, apart from open fires.

Edward VII, then prince, stayed there with his princess, Alexandra,

A nineteenth-century drawing of Haigh Hall. LRO DP 291/20.

The view from Haigh Hall of the surrounding countryside. Down there runs the canal. The distinctive chimneys marking the old pit are gone.

The start of the rocky road which leads to the last surviving row of houses which existed at the time of James Barton. This is the route he would take to and from the pit where he was murdered. On the left of the picture is George Lowton's house.

in 1873 and this required that the entire hall be decorated and carpeted afresh at a cost of £80,000. There were many servants and when carpets needed to be cleaned, twelve people were dragged them out and beat them on the lawns. Twelve grooms and coachmen attended twenty horses and the estate was self-supporting. Within it were forty farms.

When, at the end of the nineteenth century, the hall installed an electricity plant, its 124 storage batteries represented a larger number than that possessed by Wigan Corporation.

It is apparent, then, that the grandeur of the architecture was matched by the aspirations of those who produced it and enjoyed it. When those people left, Haigh Hall's soul departed with them.

JUST over a little hump-backed canal bridge in Haigh, at a house built in 1734, lives George Lowton, 76, and he is one of the few around with any intimate knowledge of the affairs of 1863.

His father worked for a time at the hall, and George remembers going there when it was necessary to move snow from a flat roof (to save it from damage from the weight). He was in the habit of playing football in company with the then earl on Sunday mornings. The place was "gorgeous" and was sold to the corporation in 1947 for £18,000, an incredibly small sum.

He was born in Barker's Cottage, close by the old Button Pit: "You'd pass the pit late at night and people would say: 'Owd Barton will be popping out and having you.' "

Once, there were three rows of houses, two of which were removed. James Barton lived in Top Row.

The three pit chimneys were landmarks and he would judge them to be 150 to 180 feet high. It was an event when they were knocked down and, with others, he was allowed out of school to watch the felling. A fire was set to the base of one, and when that fell, it demolished the other two because they were in line. The boiler holes were there for some time afterwards, and one by one the bricks disappeared as people turned up to take them for their own use. The big stones became a retaining wall at Upholland. They are still there.

The pit site is marked now only by a long drive leading to an extensively developed modern house; a bend in that thoroughfare marks the spot. All trace of the pit has gone. Once, George Lowton knew two of the Barton family, but they are dead now.

Occasionally, people turn up to inquire about the murder, and pass on. I found myself, in February, 1988, knocking on the same door (though neither of us saw the other) as Barton's great-great-great granddaughter, Joan Szymanowski, of Leigh, in Lancashire, who was reported in the local newspaper to be seeking old Barton's watch – "handed down through generations of my family, but now gone missing." This inquiry revealed the present owner, a collector, living near Wigan, and she was subsequently to give me considerable – and valuable – help and advice.

The maker, Robert Croskell, is not to be confused with Robert Roskell, who was responsible for a large variety of watches, signed both "Liverpool" and "London". Roskell worked from 1798 to 1830, and had a liking for gold dials, variously coloured, and cases with bands of stylised floral decoration. Quality varied a good deal. It would appear that the company continued in business after Roskell's death in 1830.

Missing, yet, is a cast of Thomas Grime's head made "for scientific purposes" by a phrenologist named Frederick Bridges, of Liverpool. Bridges no doubt stared at his souvenir long and hard after his initial summary, which noted – ludicrously, we might think – that "the absolute size of the brain was about average, but the animal propensities were in great excess of the moral qualities."

Bridges judged Grime to be of very low class, with ears standing at an angle of 45 degrees – a bad sign, apparently, the average being 25 degrees.

He added, "In all the murderers I have seen for the past 30 years, I have found their ears placed at angles of 35 to 45 degrees, the average being 40 degrees." On that note of mild lunacy, matters were concluded.

THE BURNING of James Barton long ago passed out of memory and into history, and it is for history to judge, as Baron Martin and his jury did before it, the guilt or otherwise of Thomas Grime, and with the same limitation: that it can judge only on what it is told, and not what it sees. Those who saw are those who knew. Those who knew are beyond testimony. The verdict, if you have read thus far, is yours to make. And your guess, no doubt, has as much merit as anyone else's, living or dead.

Note on the illustrations

The illustration of Kirkdale Gaol is reproduced by kind permission of Liverpool City Libraries. The Ordnance Survey map and the drawing of Haigh Hall (DP 291/20) have been reproduced by kind permission of the County Archivist, Lancashire County Records Office.

The line drawings in the book are the original work of Mr Bob Mann. He has studied and taught the art and design of the Victorian era and in these drawings has employed a collage technique, using and redrawing contemporary illustrations in an attempt to give an authentic pictorial description of some of the scenes in the story. For example, the cover illustration is based on documentary evidence and a study of surviving Lancashire boilers at a mill at Trawden, while the costumes have been based on some of those depicted in the *Illustrated London News* for the relevent period.